CITIZEN KEN

Citizen Ken

John Carvel

CHATTO & WINDUS · THE HOGARTH PRESS

LONDON

Published in 1984 by
Chatto & Windus · The Hogarth Press
40 William IV Street
London WC2N 4DF

British Library Cataloguing in Publication Data

Carvel, John
    Citizen Ken.
    1. Livingstone, Ken
    2. Politicians –
    England – London – Biography
    I. Title
    942.1085'092'4   DA676.8.L5

    ISBN 0-7011-3929-3
    ISBN 0-7011-3930-7 Pbk

Photoset by Rowland Phototypesetting Ltd
Bury St Edmunds, Suffolk
Printed in Great Britain by
Redwood Burn Ltd
Trowbridge, Wiltshire

Contents

To Florence and two Roberts

Preface

This book has grown out of my work for the *Guardian* since January 1981, when I was assigned to cover local government. The subject had taken on greater political importance because of efforts by Conservative Ministers to impose their will on local authorities and force them to make spending cuts. I observed at close quarters the development of the Greater London Council as one of the main bases of resistance to these policies and the monetarist philosophy which lay behind them. I saw how its leader, Ken Livingstone, survived the intense pressures of his early months in office by virtue of an unshakable self-confidence and instinctive political flair. More than any other politician of his generation, he captured the attention of the nation and shifted public debate on to ground of his own choosing.

Although it is too soon to write the definitive biography of a politician who is not yet forty (and, perhaps more to the point, is not yet even in Parliament), I decided that I was witnessing a phenomenon which deserved to be recorded and explained. While reporting the GLC, I had developed a working relationship with Livingstone: he was a source of information which, on the whole, I found to be true; and I wrote reports which, on the whole, he found to be accurate. Between Easter and Christmas 1983 he gave me a series of lengthy tape-recorded interviews, averaging about one a week, to build up his side of the story which appears in this book. I meanwhile had parallel discussions on and off the record with his political friends and enemies, council officials, relations and acquaintances who could provide different perspectives, ranging from deep affection to vitriolic loathing. It is the nature of a biography that it centres the world around its subject. Many of the people who helped me with opinions and information have political ambitions of their own and are heartily sick of Livingstone's ability to hog the limelight. I thank them for indulging my interest in his career at the expense of their own.

I regard my main debt, however, as being to the *Guardian*, which put me in a position to write this book and tolerated the distraction it caused to my daily journalistic output. The paper's news editor, Peter Cole, provided me with encouragement by day and its production team with company by night as the task proceeded. Jenny Rathbone, Richard Gott and my parents have jointly and severally given me homes to live in and desks to write at during this period. Jo Andrews, Anne McDermid, Anne Mc-Hardy, Frankie Rickford and Tony Travers were similarly generous with their time and expertise. My thanks go to them, to Annette Mills who produced many immaculate interview transcripts, to Maggie Conlin, who helped with the manuscript, to Ethel Livingstone who raided the family album to provide pictures of the young Ken, and to Jak and other cartoonists who contributed their distinctive versions of the man he turned into.

The biggest input has come from Ken Livingstone himself, who gave freely of his time without asking for any control of the eventual product. Although he has read the manuscript to check that I have not misquoted him, he has made no attempt to challenge my judgments and criticism. The rest is down to me.

JOHN CARVEL
JANUARY 1984

1 · Phew What a Caucus . . .

On GLC election night in May 1981, Ken Livingstone's supporters got a taste of what was in store within seconds of the result
being declared for his own constituency of Paddington. It seemed
that Porchester Hall, where his votes were being counted, was the
focus of more media attention than had ever been lavished on
anything to do with local government.

As the TV arc lights dimmed and Livingstone stepped down
from the platform to mingle with reporters, photographers and
party workers, he was seized by two burly men whom he had never
met and did not recognise. They picked him up by the elbows,
carried him through the crowd and bundled him into a waiting
car.

BBC Television had left nothing to chance. In the Election
Special studio David Dimbleby and Robert Mackenzie were
waiting to ask him what they thought was the most important
question of the night. Labour had won London: now who was to
lead Labour?

The episode, trivial enough in itself, was a pointer to the coming
months of media frenzy which were to turn Livingstone into a
national political figure and London's County Hall into the stage
set for a political soap opera. Livingstone says that he told the BBC
he would go to their studio when he had finished at the count. 'But
they just picked me bodily up and carried me through to get me
there on time. They didn't even ask my consent. I was really quite
put out.'

Put out – or tickled pink? As would happen so often in the next
two years, he played along with the demands which the broad-
casters and journalists made of him. It was the beginning of a
love-hate relationship with reporters on which the man's fame and
perhaps even his political power came to be based.

On this occasion the BBC's interest was understandable.

Labour had gone into the GLC campaign under the leadership of Andrew McIntosh, a 46-year-old market research executive who had won a narrow majority in the Labour group elections the year before. Relying largely on right-wing support, he had defeated Livingstone in the final ballot by a majority of one vote, with two abstentions. It had been common knowledge during the 1981 campaign that Livingstone, the 35-year-old left-winger, would be mounting a challenge to McIntosh's leadership as soon as the newly-elected group of councillors assembled, enlarged by the expected crop of Labour gains.

The GLC Conservative leader, Sir Horace Cutler, had made much political capital out of the charge that the Labour left were about to hijack London. They were trying to win the vote behind the comfortable image of nice Mr McIntosh, but then they would ditch him in favour of the sinister Livingstone. 'The Marxist threat to London is no figment of the imagination,' warned the Tory GLC manifesto. 'The old Labour Party has gone. Herbert Morrison [the inter-war Labour leader of the former London County Council] would turn in his grave at the sight of today's Labour Party, which is dominated by Marxists and extremists.' Within the sixteen pages of this short manifesto, Marx and Marxists were mentioned seventeen times. And a week before polling day, in an article in the *Daily Express* headlined WHY WE MUST STOP THESE RED WRECKERS, Cutler thundered that the aim of the extremists was to 'establish a Marxist power-base in London from which support can be given to the wider movement to take over the Labour Party: and from which a concerted effort can be made to unseat the Government of the day – even a Labour Government if it puts nation before party.'

This was a period of major advances by the left within the Labour Party. A series of party conferences since Labour's general election defeat in May 1979 had changed the constitutional rules to satisfy leftist pressure for mandatory reselection of Parliamentary candidates (to give constituency parties the power to discard sitting MPs) and for a new electoral college to choose the party leader (previously the prerogative of MPs themselves). The campaign to win Tony Benn the deputy leadership of the party,

Livingstone and Andrew McIntosh face to face at County Hall, May 8, 1981, hours before Livingstone took over the leadership (*Guardian*)

Sir Horace Cutler, Tory GLC Leader, forecasts his defeat
(*Press Association*)

which came within one per cent of victory at Brighton in September 1981, was also already gathering momentum.

In this context, Livingstone's challenge exerted a fascination on politicians and the media. Just as he saw a left-led Labour GLC as a testbed of more red-blooded socialist policies for a future Labour government, so he was seen as the pioneer of tactics by which the left could eventually seize power in Westminster – winning a majority under a 'traditional' leader and then ditching him or her once power was secured. Since few people in the press or the Parliamentary Labour Party favoured either the policies or the tactics, Livingstone fitted snugly into the category of 'extremist', a platoon leader of the advance party of Bennite shock troops.

His platoon was not the only one in the field on that local election night in May 1981. With varying degrees of left-wing strength, Labour groups were winning a clean sweep of power throughout the English metropolitan counties. Conservative administrations were defeated in Merseyside, Greater Manchester, West Yorkshire and the West Midlands; and Labour strengthened its grip on South Yorkshire and Tyne and Wear. In the shires, where Labour had been devastated by a Tory landslide in the previous elections of 1977, Labour won control of Northumberland, Cumbria, Lancashire, Humberside, Derbyshire, Nottinghamshire, Staffordshire and Avon. It also deprived the Tories of overall majorities in Bedfordshire, Berkshire, Cheshire, Leicestershire and Northamptonshire.

Television viewers learned little of this; indeed the 'national' programme on which Livingstone was to appear gave scant attention to any results outside London. This was due to the second reason for Livingstone's projection to political stardom – the metropolitan bias of national news reporting. Although the BBC is not usually as extravagantly London-oriented as most of the press, it gave the impression that night that nothing outside the capital merited analysis. Almost all the men and women controlling the national media live in London or within commuting distance of it; and, with some honourable exceptions, most of their programmes and newspapers let it show.

The phenomenon of a left-wing administration seizing control of an important local authority was not something new. In Sheffield, for instance, the city council under David Blunkett's leadership had already been pursuing policies which were just as left-wing as anything Livingstone had to offer. What is more, Sheffield metropolitan district council had far more power to make an impact on its area because, unlike the GLC, it had responsibility for a wider range of activities, including housing and social services. Blunkett – two years younger than Livingstone, blind, charismatic and with a revivalist style of socialist oratory which none of his contemporaries could emulate – would have attracted huge national controversy if his centre of operations had not been 150 miles away from London. As it was, the media merely cracked jokes about the People's Republic of Sheffield and more or less let him get on with it.

The short point is that Livingstone became an immediate national figure not only because he was a left-winger, but also because he operated in London. And the question of the moment on the night of May 7, 1981, was: would he have enough support to win the leadership of the GLC?

In spite of his confidence in front of cameras, he himself wasn't sure. 'I arrived in the studios just in time to hear Shirley Williams slagging me off,' he says. 'We had a bit of questioning. Then they turned to Bob Mackenzie.' The late Robert Mackenzie was a professor of politics who had turned himself into a TV celebrity by the use of a cardboard toy called a 'swingometer' which he brought out on election nights to measure the number of seats parties would win or lose for given percentage changes in national political opinion. On that occasion he had turned his analytic powers to the political complexion of the new GLC. 'I have been doing a study of GLC members and my analysis of the people elected tonight shows that if the left-wing want to, they have got the votes to get rid of Mr McIntosh and put in Mr Livingstone,' Mackenzie said.

That was the arithmetic Livingstone had been working for throughout the period since Labour's defeat at the general election in May 1979. When he learned that he had won in Paddington by 2,397 votes, he had calculated that Labour would gain 57 or 58

of the 92 GLC seats. That should have brought him home and
dry. But, probably thanks to their media exposure, Livingstone in
Paddington and McIntosh in Tottenham had both done better
than the general swing to Labour. Livingstone's close colleague,
Ted Knight, leader of Lambeth council, had been surprisingly
beaten in Norwood after a bitter campaign against his council's
recent supplementary rate demand. Labour also failed to win
Hampstead and a handful of other marginals in which Livingstone
supporters had been candidates. 'After the television, I trundled
off to do some radio interviews,' he says. 'But as the results came
through, I became decidedly nervous for the first time since
the previous July that we might not have the votes to do it.
What it meant was that there was not going to be anything like the
number of left-wingers that there should have been. The proportion of the left if we won sixty seats was better than if we won
fifty. If the centre had wanted to, it could have kept Andrew in
power.'

In the forty-eight hours before polling Livingstone had button-
holed or phoned all Labour candidates who might win and might
vote for him in the leadership ballot. He had asked them to attend
a left caucus meeting on the day after the poll. (The operation was
kept secret for fear of the mileage the Tories would have made of it
in the final day of the campaign.) So, as he moved on from the
broadcasting stations to catch the tail end of his supporters' party
in Paddington, he knew that there was nothing more that could be
done that night. By about three a.m. he got back to his bedsitter in
Maida Vale. As he pored over the results yet again, he became
depressed about the reasons for Ted Knight's defeat in Norwood.
Could this same unpopularity attach itself to a left-wing GLC?
Was this what would happen when the GLC brought in the
supplementary rate implied in its plans for London Transport? He
went to sleep with doubt in his mind.

Meanwhile McIntosh was behaving as if his personal victory
was assured. He too put in his television appearances before
repairing in the early hours to a celebration party at County Hall
with the Labour leader Michael Foot, the Parliamentary chief
whip Michael Cocks, and McIntosh's deputy, Illtyd Harrington.

The whisky bottles were brought out and, according to Harrington, Foot toasted McIntosh's success with the memorably mistaken prophesy: 'It's going to be fine because you, Andrew, are in charge and you know the machine.' Within fifteen hours the man who knew the machine was going to be flattened by it.

McIntosh appears to have been genuinely ignorant of the fate that was in store for him. He had done his count and says he believed he would win by two or three votes. When he arrived at County Hall the next morning, determined to take a businesslike grip on power, he carried with him a letter from Foot endorsing his leadership. This was to be his trump card in winning over waverers in the group. He summoned the chief officers and told them his immediate priorities for action. Then he gave a press conference to tell the world: 'I am going to win. The results of the election show that the people of London wanted the Labour Party to win, but they also wanted a Labour administration of responsible and realistic people. That is what they are going to get.' Due largely to this manifest confidence the *Standard*, London's evening paper, led with the headline THE LEFT LOSE OUT under a strapline 'Red Ted defeated: Moderates "in control".'

But McIntosh was not in control. He had been outmanoeuvred by the left on every key piece of preparation. He had not organised to ensure that his supporters won party selection battles in the London marginals. He had done nothing to woo the old-guard members of the Labour centre (except Harrington) or even to leave them cause to hope that they might get a job in his new administration. And he had failed to block Livingstone's plans to fix the timetable for the group elections to give maximum impetus to the left.

McIntosh's idea had been to hold the Labour group meeting at nine a.m. on the day after the poll, to have his leadership confirmed and then to take the weekend to work out his administration which the group would be asked to ratify the following week. But Livingstone got his sympathisers on the London Labour Party regional executive, which was responsible for convening the meeting, to fix it for five p.m. This was arranged on the somewhat bogus argument that it might take that long to complete any recounts in close-fought constituencies. That gave him scope to call his caucus meeting at a reasonable time in the afternoon when everyone was ready for action after the revelries of the night before.

'We needed two hours for all the new incoming left people to sit down and argue out what we were going to do about everything. There had been a not greatly debated consensus that I would stand against Andrew,' says Livingstone. 'Beyond that nothing was really firm. What I needed to do was to make sure that we welded together the existing members here who were prepared to vote to remove Andrew with the incoming people. There could easily have been a split between those two groups.'

Livingstone says it is incorrect to call the meeting a left caucus. 'It was basically everybody who was prepared to see a change of Andrew's leadership for mine. So it was people who would be called hard left, soft left and centre and a couple of people on the right who decided they wanted to come and sit in.'

Livingstone's account of the controversial meeting in room 166 at County Hall is as follows: 'We walked into the room and by the time we started a majority of the next Labour group were there. That was a tremendous boost to confidence. People who might have had doubts or reservations suddenly could see that we did have the votes to do it.

'I said what I thought had gone wrong in the past and why I thought we should have a change now. Illtyd Harrington said I should stand for the leadership and there was a general murmur of agreement. Then we had a long debate about whether or not we should elect me as leader and then defer everything else until people could go back to their local parties and talk about who were the candidates for particular posts.

'We decided that, as it was necessary to start changing the building quickly, we couldn't wait five or six weeks for that and we would therefore have to go straight into all the other elections. So we sat round the table: I went through all the list of posts and asked if anyone was interested in standing. Where more than one wanted to stand, they each made a little speech and the caucus decided which they wanted to support. There were an awful lot of contested posts. People that I hadn't expected to do things wanted to do them . . .'

The caucus broke up at four forty-five with a full slate of candidates agreed. It had been attended by two-thirds of the fifty Labour councillors elected the day before.

When the full group assembled at five, things were still going wrong for McIntosh. He passed up to George Page, the London Labour Party regional secretary, his letter of support from Foot, expecting him to read it out at the start of the meeting. Page stayed silent. 'The entire regional staff, who no one can say are exactly Militant-dominated, were on my side,' says Livingstone. 'They felt in simple party terms that I was the politician who knew how to work the Labour Party and Andrew wasn't.

'It seems silly, but one of Andrew's major mistakes was to go to the regional executive with flip charts and give them lectures on what was to be done. He gave them market research presentations. They felt that they were being treated like kids at school. He did it three times. It was the kiss of death.'

So the group moved straight to the leadership election with a victory for Livingstone by thirty votes to twenty. Only two-thirds of his support could be described as left-wing. McIntosh was shattered. He had prepared no list of right-wing candidates for the other important committee chairmanships. So the meeting went on to elect the entire left caucus slate. The whole proceedings took no more than forty minutes before Livingstone emerged to begin three hours of interviews with the media. The next day the left carried out a parallel coup on the Inner London Education Authority (made up of GLC and borough councillors) where the previous Labour leader, Sir Ashley Bramall, was deposed by Bryn Davies. On Sunday night, as the left were holding a celebratory party at the home of one of the new Labour councillors, Valerie Wise, the news came through that Mitterrand had been elected president in France. For a while at least it seemed that everything was for the best in the best of all possible leftist worlds.

Livingstone's victory gave Fleet Street a field day. RED KEN CROWNED KING OF LONDON, said the *Sun*. 'Red Ken ousted moderate Andrew McIntosh, 46, in a private poll by the 50 newly elected councillors. His victory means full-steam-ahead red-blooded Socialism for London,' its reporters explained. The *Daily Mail* news story said: 'A left-wing extremist was installed as leader of the Greater London Council yesterday, less than 24 hours after Labour won control . . . And last night the signs were that the Left's victory in London could be repeated up and down the country where Labour has won control of county halls. Mr Livingstone's election came as Mrs Thatcher was warning in a speech at Perth that extremists were busy manipulating Labour's membership to gain power. She said that they had one purpose: 'To impose upon this nation a tyranny which the peoples of Eastern Europe yearn to cast aside." '

The *Daily Express* commented that the Labour group's decision displayed 'their contempt for the voters' by unceremoniously ditching McIntosh in favour of 'the political extremist Ken Livingstone'. It listed some of his left-wing credentials and raised a theme which was to become a running criticism in the press. 'For the last six years and more he has had no proper job. Instead he has

Sunday Express, May 10, 1981

acted as a professional local councillor, living on his "expenses" of about £7,000 a year.' (Unlike those journalists who live on their expenses, councillors have scales of remuneration laid down by Parliament. Livingstone was actually earning only £3,000.)

By Monday the *Standard* was commenting:

The worst nightmares about the Greater London Council and its new masters on the far left seem to be coming true even faster than we had feared. Mr Ken Livingstone and his fellows have steamrollered their more moderate (and experienced) colleagues out of the way in record time . . . The truth which the Left will never acknowledge is that they are operating on a non-existent mandate. Labour won the election under the moderate Mr McIntosh (and small thanks he got). The Left's best-known candidate, Mr Ted Knight, was rejected out of hand by the voters of Lambeth, against the tide everywhere else. So now it is up to the Government and, in particular to Mr Michael Heseltine (the Environment Secretary), Mr William Whitelaw (Home Secretary) and Mr Mark Carlisle (Education Secretary) to keep some measure of control over London's spending, policing and education . . .

But it was not only in the right-wing press that Livingstone's coup was criticised. Three days after the group meeting the *Guardian* and the *Mirror* carried lengthy reports of complaints by McIntosh that he had been ousted by means of an illegitimate form of caucus rule. McIntosh told the *Mirror*: 'The danger to the Labour Party is so great that I have decided I must expose what is going on. It's gang warfare – just like the Jets and the Sharks. The left are after personal power.'

McIntosh complained that a handful of left-wingers held a secret meeting in a pub the week before the election at which Livingstone, Ted Knight and others who were not even candidates drew up a list of left-wingers for major committee posts. McIntosh alleged that the left won sufficient support by persuading moderates to back them in return for jobs. 'I don't object to my personal defeat – that's part of politics. But I am objecting violently to what I call the Russian doll strategy, whereby a small secret group of self-selected people organise to impose their will on a larger group. If it becomes the pattern of future elections, the Labour Party is in very serious trouble.'

A *Mirror* editorial argued: 'If a small, unelected group can impose its will on a larger, elected one which, in turn, dominates an even bigger group which runs a city, that is not open government, nor democracy. It is deception.'

The result of all this ballyhoo was further to elevate media interest in the GLC – already evident on election night. The GLC in general and Livingstone in particular became newsworthy. No matter that the Livingstone administration set out to implement exactly the same manifesto policies to which McIntosh was also committed. No matter that it had to operate within the narrow band of functions which the GLC was legally permitted to perform. As far as news editors were concerned, 'Red Ken' switched from being a minor bore in the big yawn of local government into a public figure who merited the sort of coverage which MPs crave and never get.

But how much justice is there in McIntosh's charge that something unseemly happened on Livingstone's road to leadership victory? It is, on the face of it, unsatisfactory that the voters should elect a party to power under one leader only to find him replaced within twenty-four hours by his internal party opponent.

In the subtle blend of factors which influence peoples' votes, trust in a party's leader is plausibly just as important as studied appraisal of its policies. It can hardly be argued that Livingstone's victory was a surprise, since the possibility was one of the main thrusts of the Conservative campaign. But Livingstone acknowledges that switching leaders in this way is undesirable if it can be avoided. He says he tried to persuade McIntosh to step down a few months before the election on the grounds that a Livingstone victory was inevitable: 'But Andrew thought I was mad.' He also pushed for rule changes which would have given the London Labour Party conference the job of electing the GLC leader, but this idea was scotched by Labour's National Executive Committee (NEC).

It seems unreasonable to expect parties to draw up rules to prevent them changing leaders after elections. The leader of a council needs to have the confidence of his group. And if, as happened at the GLC elections in 1981, that group is doubled in size as a result of an election, the new members deserve just as much of a say as the old ones.

McIntosh's complaint is directed not at the fact there was an election which he happened to lose, but at the way in which it was conducted. The theoretical objection to decisions by caucus is that the will of the majority can be flouted. Say there are one hundred people entitled to choose a leader or Parliamentary candidate. The result could be determined by a majority of fifty-one of them. If these fifty-one meet separately to make a choice, which they all agree they will be bound by, the eventual outcome can be decided by only twenty-six people. This smaller group could itself be influenced by the activities of a closed inner caucus or by secret deals between individuals. So, theoretically, a tiny group of people could manipulate the eventual result. This is why caucuses are banned in the selection procedure for Labour Parliamentary candidates, as Livingstone was to learn to his cost in his abortive bid to become candidate for the Brent East constituency at the 1983 general election.

In the case of the GLC leadership election, the three p.m. caucus meeting was not secret. It was open to right-wingers to attend – and at least one overt McIntosh supporter sat through the whole proceedings. The left did try to change the rules in the eventual group meeting to remove the secrecy of the leadership ballot. If they had succeeded, this could have increased the pressure on waverers in the centre to vote as the caucus directed. But the left failed to get the two-thirds majority it needed to make this change in the rules. This made it possible for councillors to promise their votes to Livingstone, but actually vote for McIntosh. Several did.

So McIntosh's objections to the procedures are reduced to two allegations. First that an inner caucus of the left pre-arranged its slate of major committee chairmanships. And second that the waverers in the 'venal' centre were bribed to vote left by the offer of posts in the Livingstone administration.

Livingstone's answer is that he was not in a position to deliver jobs to people. 'Lots of them had said to me they were going to stand for particular things. I made certain not to get involved in that, because had I started to do it, it would have been counter-productive. The people you weren't offering the job to would end up voting for someone else. As soon as you started that it would be all round the building anyhow . . . The real effort had been endlessly talking to people who were going to be elected saying, we cannot come in and sweep everything out of the way and have a completely new machine. We have got to weld together and build the widest possible basis of support there. That meant you had got to have people who had already voted for me at the previous election carried with us in the change.'

The two key figures here were Illtyd Harrington, who was re-elected deputy leader, and Harvey Hinds, who continued as chief whip. Both had switched their support to Livingstone in 1980 when Harrington's own leadership bid was defeated at the first ballot. They had it in their influence to make either McIntosh or Livingstone leader in 1981; and the fact that Livingstone backed them in the caucus for senior jobs can probably fairly be said to be more the consequence of their support than its cause. The surprise in all this is not that politicians make arrangements with each other, but that McIntosh did so little to stitch up his own coalition of support. 'I am constitutionally incapable of running two battles at the same time,' he says. 'I was concentrating on winning the election . . . That took 105 per cent of my time. Afterwards I had no opportunity to change.'

The political epitaph to McIntosh, a resident of the north London village of Highgate, was recorded by the Conservative leader, Sir Horace Cutler, at the first meeting of the new council:

> There lived a man on Highgate Mount.
> He won the votes but did not count.

In 1983, on Michael Foot's recommendation, McIntosh entered the House of Lords.

To understand why the left won power and what it did with it, it is first necessary to pick up three strands. The reason why the older men of the centre were ready to link up with the younger and more abrasive men and women of the left was based in their dissatisfac-

LONDON LABOUR BRIEFING 20p

No 11   JUNE   1981

SPECIAL VICTORY ISSUE!

LONDON'S OURS!

Ken Livingstone
GLC Leader

After the most vicious GLC election campaign of all time, Labour has won a working majority on a radical socialist programme. The torrent of Macarthy-style red-baiting and gross distortion of the cost of Labour's programme – coupled with extensive media coverage – left no-one in any doubt that this GLC election was the trial run for the next general election campaign. The results need to be seen in this light.

We are not just talking about another mid-term council election showing the normal anti-government swing. Voters in Paddington, where I was the candidate, responded to the campaign on firm class lines. The Social Democractic candidate was crushed, with under 7 per cent of the vote. His only impact was in the safe Tory areas of Hyde Park and Lancaster Gate. In Islington North we won our third highest swing to Labour – clear proof that the SDP took its vote from the Tories.

Rates

The only problem in the campaign was the difficult issue of rates. The emphasis we placed on the need to increase rates was honestly put, but we failed to go on to the attack against the Government on this issue. Our central demand should have been for the restoration of the £300 million Rate Support Grant which Heseltine stole from London. From now on, this demand will be at the centre of our on-going campaign against the Government.

We will go into the constituencies with Tory MPs and lead the demand that they vote in Parliament to restore our Rate Support Grant and Housing programme cuts. Where they refuse, we shall publish their voting records and demand their removal.

We will be working with the NEC's Home Policy Committee to prepare detailed legislation for the next Labour Government. No-one will be left in any doubt that the GLC is now a campaigning organ and a bastion of power for the labour movement within a national context.

Now for the Government

The Regional Executive, London Labour MPs and Local Government Committees will be drawn into the plans for the fight ahead. There is no doubt that the party was damaged in Lambeth and Camden by the supplementary rates which were forced on those councils by the Auditor and Heseltine. We must avoid being trapped in the same way. We must ensure that we plan the way ahead rather than just respond to the Government's attacks as they occur. Part of our task will be to sustain a holding operation until such time as the Tory Government can be brought down and replaced by a left-wing Labour

Continued next page

Labour—Take the Power!

tion with a history of authoritarian Labour leadership at the GLC. The reason why the left was organised for power lay in the work done by Livingstone and others in welding together a broad left alliance around a magazine called *London Labour Briefing*. And the reason why it was Livingstone who took the lead in this endeavour was the result of the political awakening of the son of Tory parents who grew up in the relatively prosperous environment of south London after the war.

2 · Spawning Grounds

Livingstone was a slow starter. He is a qualified teacher who failed his eleven-plus; a conviction politician who left school without firm political views; a Labour leader who did not join the party (or any other) until the age of twenty-three.

He is also the product of an age of weakening class loyalties. His formative years were those of Harold Macmillan and never-had-it-so-good. He is the son of parents who, by dint of hard work and Victorian values, advanced themselves to become owner-occupiers and to enjoy a standard of living and security which their forbears had never known. This is not the conventional pedigree of socialism.

Previous generations of Labour leaders have been able to root their beliefs in their experiences as children either sharing or observing the sufferings of the working class. This seemed at least to give them political ballast. The voters thought they could fathom where these politicians were going because they knew where they had come from. But life has changed. Among the Labour left there is a great sense of betrayal that leaders from Ramsay MacDonald to Harold Wilson have been strong on background but weak on principle. So politicians are now being measured by the constancy and ability with which they project their beliefs and not by the weight of their pedigrees. You do not hear the left-wing credentials of Tony Benn challenged because of his personal financial security or inherited (and disclaimed) peerage. Nor is the resolution of the Conservative Cabinet doubted because of its diminished quotient of old Etonians. Indeed the reverse seems to be true.

The fascinating question raised by this trend towards conviction politics is how these convictions materialise. In the case of Ken Livingstone, the answer was slowly.

He was born on June 17, 1945, just after the Allied victory in

Europe, but before the Second World War ended in the Japanese theatre with the nuclear explosions at Hiroshima and Nagasaki. His mother, Ethel, was an acrobatic dancer who had gone on the stage at the age of fourteen and toured the provincial music halls, mostly in a three-woman act called the Kenleigh Sisters. They did many of the tricks now associated with gymnastics competitors, backflips, splits and balancing acts, often followed by some tap dancing and perhaps a little ballet. She also performed in circuses in an act that involved skilful balancing tricks on ladders on the top of elephants. In spite of frequent offers, she always turned down speaking parts.

His father, Bob, was a merchant seaman who survived several days adrift in the Irish Sea after being torpedoed on a wartime run to Murmansk. They had met on a Tuesday night in April 1940 at a music hall in Workington where Ethel was performing alongside the Great Lyle, an illusionist who purported to saw people in half. Bob was with two of his shipmates in the front row during the performance. They were on shore leave, had already had a few drinks, and were making rather a nuisance of themselves waving and winking at Ethel and her two fellow artistes as they went through their act. At the interval the men slipped a message through to them via one of the show's comedians, inviting them out for a meal afterwards. Ethel had only recently broken off another relationship and, at the time, was feeling rather hostile to men in general; but the others were keen and, to make up the pairs, she went along. It was during the blackout and the only place to eat in Workington was a fish and chip shop.

Ethel and Bob hit it off instantly. She recalls: 'We were chatting away and then he started singing and he had a voice very much like Bing Crosby. He sang "I have eyes to see with, but they see only you". It was a lovely number. And he really meant it. We were meant to meet.' With Bob away at sea and Ethel on tour, they saw each other only three times over the next three months and then got married.

Ethel's father had been killed in the First World War and she and her brother were brought up by her mother in a succession of private rented flats between Kennington and Mitcham in south

London. Bob was born in Dunoon in western Scotland. His family had emigrated to Argentina, but came back to Scotland for the birth so that he would not be obliged to serve in the Argentine armed forces when he grew up. He was brought up in Argentina until the age of seven and then returned again to Scotland, where his mother died when he was fourteen. The family disintegrated and he went to live with his sister until he was sixteen, when he joined the Merchant Marine. Ethel and Bob were both twenty-five when they met. The stability of their marriage gave their children the background of two-parent domestic harmony which they themselves had lacked. Ken Livingstone says: 'They were still very much in love right the way through their life together. Most of my contemporaries at school had parents who seemed to have fallen into a state of either armed neutrality or resigned boredom. They were quite unusual in the sense that they were still very much in love. They had actually met and clicked instantly.'

Ken was their first child. He was born in Ethel's mother's flat at 21b Shrubbery Road, opposite the police station in Streatham. By one of life's strange coincidences, he suffered from exactly the same post-natal condition as Herbert Morrison, the only local government politician before Livingstone to become a household name. Both Morrison and Livingstone got infections because their midwives failed to clean out their eyes properly at birth. In Morrison's case it caused the permanent loss of one eye. By the time Livingstone was born, medical science had advanced and the doctors prescribed drops which cleared up the mass of yellow pus which disfigured his infant features.

Ethel recalls that he looked so awful as a new-born baby, with his bad eye and total lack of hair, that she covered him up when she took him out for walks. 'I thought he looked ugly, so I used to put the blankets over his head and tell people not to disturb him. He looked terribly ill for the first few weeks, but he was lovely by the time he was six months.' The baby was christened Kenneth Robert. His sister, Lin, was born two and a half years later.

Their father Bob went back to sea as a trawlerman and was away for long periods. Much as he loved Ethel, he could not take living with her strongly possessive mother. Livingstone recalls: 'My

Bob, Ethel and Ken Livingstone, Butlin's, Skegness, summer 1947 (*Ethel Livingstone*)

Ken pedals out on his own, Skegness, summer 1947 (*Ethel Livingstone*)

Young Ken shows his teeth, aged 4 (*Ethel Livingstone*)

Ken, 5, and his sister Lin, 2½, Brockwell Park, 1950 (*Ethel Livingstone*)

mum started pestering the old London County Council for a home of her own, because living with us in one room at my grandmother's place was no joy. And eventually about 1950 they got an offer on the new Tulse Hill estate and moved in there.'

Although this estate was to deteriorate badly in the 1970s, it was initially very attractive. The Livingstone family stayed there until 1957, when they managed to buy their own house in west Norwood. 'My parents really had to struggle to get the deposit and the mortgage. After my father stopped doing the trawler fishing, he used to be a window cleaner during the day and in the evenings he worked on shifting stage scenery at the Streatham Hill Theatre when Streatham was still suburban enough to sustain an arts theatre. My mum used usually to work serving at the bakers, Broomfields – she eventually became manageress – and in the evenings she used to work at the cinema as an usherette. My gran used to stop with us and look after us as kids. They really worked hard all the time.'

From 1955 Ethel started saving all her £4-a-week wages to provide the £400 deposit they needed for a house of their own. By the time she had saved the money, the cost of the deposit had risen to £500, but the estate agent lent them the extra £100 out of his own pocket. They moved into a big old three-storey house at 66 Wolfington Road, West Norwood.

The young Ken was always an outgoing child, with a desire to hold the centre of the stage. His mother recalls that when she collected him from his first day at St Leonard's Infants School, the teacher reported that he had kept the whole class amused all afternoon by talking and singing and doing little acts.

The Livingstone family almost always earned enough money to go on annual holidays to the south coast, the Isle of Wight, or up to Dunoon to stay with relatives. They went to the cinema two or three times a week and got their first television in 1956. Livingstone's first political memories are of cinema newsreels of the Korean war, but at that stage there was little political discussion in the home. Both his parents held Tory party cards and his father used to man a polling station for the Conservatives on election days, but they were not activists. 'They were part of the generation of Tories who thought Churchill was excellent and have been progressively more disillusioned with each successive Tory leader,' Livingstone says. His uncle was active in Streatham Conservative association. 'But he resigned in protest when old Shrunken Glands [Duncan Sandys, Churchill's son-in-law] was imposed on them as the Tory candidate in preference to his local employer.' It sounds as if they'd all have got on a treat with Margaret Thatcher's folks in Grantham.

Livingstone's political perceptions began to shape up during Suez and the Hungarian uprising of 1956; but the stimulus came from school rather than home. At the age of eleven, he moved to Tulse Hill School, a brand new comprehensive built in the early

The Livingstones and friend, 1955 (*Ethel Livingstone*)

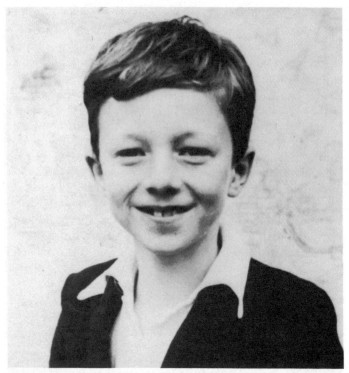

Ken, 10, while at St Leonard's Church of England Junior School (*Ethel Livingstone*)

wave of secondary education reform. Although the comprehensives were designed to end segregation of children into grammar schools for the academically bright and secondary moderns for the rest, patterns of segregation were still strongly entrenched within them. The eleven-plus exam, which separated academic sheep and goats, continued in London well into the 1960s.

Livingstone failed it, doing tolerably well on the general knowledge papers, but badly in English and maths. Tulse Hill then had a thirteen-form entry for eleven-year-olds. 'There were three forms that were considered academic, three forms that the school thought were worth worrying about, and the rest which were largely ignored.' Livingstone was put in form six at the bottom of the middle category.

It was there in his first year that Livingstone was exposed to an influence which he thinks had a 'dramatic' effect on his political development. His form master was Philip Hobsbaum, now Reader in English at Glasgow University (and a distant relation of the Marxist historian Eric Hobsbawm). 'In terms of 1956, he was positively revolutionary. He put newspapers on the classroom wall. He'd move all the desks out to the edge and we'd have an impromptu play. We'd stage a mock trial and things like that . . . For eleven-year-old kids he was incredibly larger than life, dominating, with a great beard. We'd all look up at him and he'd do outrageously exciting things – as opposed to all the other boring teachers. So we all loved him greatly. He got us to debate Suez and Hungary. We were never aware of what his own politics were, but he made us discuss politics.

Hobsbaum remembers Livingstone as one of four exceptional boys in the class whom he expected to hear of again in later life. 'He was highly articulate and very friendly, a marvellous communicator. I thought he would have a future in journalism or advertising rather than politics. At the age of eleven, he had great ability to get his points across and he was unflappable. He would always turn aside any aggression from the other boys with a joke.' Hobsbaum recalls taking the class to visit the House of Lords. 'He was completely at home there, not at all in awe of institutions or being on strange territory.'

Hobsbaum taught Livingstone only for a year. 'They shuffled round the form teachers each year, which was a real pain. But he started me arguing about politics. I then found it was a subject of endless discussion and argument at the dinner table every night, because my father had strong political views. From then on, right the way through, the amount of time I spent discussing politics built up and up . . . Yes, I became an argumentative cocky little brat.'

After the first two years, Livingstone moved, in more ways than one, into a different class. 'It was a jump I never adjusted to, because virtually all my friends in the sixth grade were working class. I then moved up into the second grade and into a form which was overwhelmingly middle class. I didn't find it a happy transition and I kept most of my friends from the sixth grade. So I was aware of class and I really didn't perceive myself as middle class. It was a gut reaction. I suppose I perceived myself as working class without really being aware of the terminology.'

By his fifth year, political discussion at school was becoming more vitriolic. 'It was the time that Colin Jordan was stomping around in jackboots. There was a large block of fascist supporters at school and another block of kids who were in, or claimed to be in, the Communist Party. I used to argue with virtually everybody and never joined anything ... Why not? Because my primary interest was natural history.'

At that stage Livingstone was spending his pocket money and the income from a paper round on building up a collection of increasingly exotic reptiles and amphibians. His mother recalls that his bedroom came to resemble a reptile house at the zoo. The family favourite was a South American bullfrog, *Leptodactylus Pentodactylus*, which they nicknamed Black Joe and which the young Ken took for walks on his shoulder, often calling in at his mother's shop to frighten the customers. As time went on he also acquired two three-foot monitor lizards (one of which terrified the household when it escaped and hid behind a chest of drawers), some salamanders, some snakes and a baby alligator which his mother unsuccessfully tried to ban from the house on the grounds that when it grew up it might eat the dogs. Once a friend lent him two extremely poisonous Formosan vipers while he went on holiday, thoughtfully providing a serum which, in the case of bites, had to be injected within two minutes to avert death.

The teenage Livingstone was a solitary young man, rarely going out after school except in the dead of night to dig up worms from neighbours' gardens to feed to his pets. He hated sport, never took to religion and seemed to have little interest in girls (except for sister Lin's friends, whom he would lure up to his room for close encounters with his frogs).

Lin remembers his love of shocking people as one of the banes of her childhood – like the time when he left her unawares on a bus after firmly tying her plaits around a metal pole. 'You could never get your own back if he decided to show you up. Nothing embarrassed him,' she says. It was a lesson that Livingstone's future political opponents were in time to learn without the compensations of close family love. Lin also dates her brother's pro-feminist perceptions from this time (in spite of the things he did to her girl friends with his frogs). 'We were always brought up as equals. There was never any question that Ken was more important than I was because he was a boy. Mum's opinion was never any less important than Dad's and Dad always did the housework. I don't think Ken has ever felt superior to women, the way a lot of men do.'

The equality was less obvious between mother and son. The young Ken often refused to eat what the rest of the family were having for dinner and made his mother prepare special home-made fishcakes or beefburgers – he wouldn't touch ready-made versions available in the shops. It was always a toss-up whether the dinner-time row between Ken and his dad would be about his exacting culinary requests or his tendency to come out with provocative political remarks designed to rile his father's Tory sensibilities.

Livingstone says that his interest in politics 'became really acute in 1960 with the American presidential election. Also the election of Pope John XXIII was quite an impact because he was one of the first public figures to come over via the medium of television as a really decent person. He made a strong impact on me. His death was the first time I cried for someone who'd died that I didn't know.'

Livingstone left school at seventeen at the end of his first year in the sixth form, with O-levels in English Literature, English Language, Art and Geography. Tulse Hill had awakened the two enthusiasms which were to dominate his life – politics and natural history. But it had failed to win his affections. 'I was a bad kid at school . . . I didn't find it a happy place after that first year with Hobsbaum. And I wasn't then happy until I left. I didn't like the restrictions. I used to bunk off quite a lot. Two or three of us would mooch around the streets for the afternoon. Or I'd go to the library and read natural history books, political books, things about China . . . The real problem is that a school with 2,100 kids cannot know where they are. I managed to avoid a whole range of things I didn't like doing at school just because I was sufficiently cunning.'

When Livingstone left Tulse Hill, he says he was politically aware, but still uncommitted. That changed when he started work in 1962 as a six-pounds-five-shillings-a-week lab technician at the Chester Beatty cancer research unit in Fulham Road.

'There were about fourteen of us technicians, all men. I suddenly dropped into an environment where everyone in that room except me was a committed socialist from a committed Labour background.' It was the time when the Macmillan government was creaking towards its close, with the Profumo scandal, the first-round attempts to get Britain into the Common Market and the emergence of Harold Wilson, the Labour leader who promised to end government from the grouse moors and regenerate Britain's economy 'in the white heat of the technological revolution'.

'It was then that my political allegiances firmed up solidly on the Labour Party side with all that naive belief that Wilson was actually going to do something.' Livingstone says he felt a 'trembling of excitement' when Wilson won in 1964, followed by a growing disillusionment over the next two or three years.

He could at this stage have become just another disaffected Labour voter, but in the winter of 1966/7 he went on a six-month hitch-hiking tour of West Africa which greatly sharpened up his political commitment. With Mick Towns, a fellow worker at the Fulham Road laboratory, he hitched through France, Spain, Morocco, Algeria and then due south to Niger and Nigeria, arriving in Lagos as the Biafran war was developing, and then on to Togo and Ghana. The trip was designed to pursue their mutual interest in natural history; and indeed for about a thousand miles of it Livingstone nursed a baby ostrich which he had saved from certain death in a local cooking pot. He hitched with it wrapped in a towel under his arm and got severe gastric problems from pre-chewing its food. The ostrich was left behind in Lagos children's zoo. But in the course of the tour Livingstone picked up a lot of less tangible experiences which he brought back home. It was a time of political ferment in West Africa, with massacres in Nigeria, a coup in Togo and recent upheavals in Ghana and Algeria.

'My six months hitch-hiking abroad had very much the impact on me that national service must have had on some other people, or going to university. It suddenly dramatically expanded my horizons. We kept meeting Peace Corps and VSO [Voluntary Service Overseas] people, young people who were leftish or at least argued a lot about politics. It just suddenly widened my horizon and gave me an awful lot more self-confidence. So I came back much more confident in my politics.'

Livingstone had given away his reptile collection before making the African trip. (His mother had put her foot down at taking on the job of feeding the snakes with live mice while he was away.) By the time he came back, his interests had become focused almost a hundred per cent on politics. In Africa he had met a group of American Peace Corps workers who wanted to avoid the draft for the Vietnam war. Livingstone got involved in trying to get them into Britain. He lobbied his local MP, John Fraser, and for the first time became a political activist in the British campaign to help the US draft resisters.

A second influence at this stage was the attitude of the Norwood Conservative candidate on race. 'My father's major philosophy had always been a strongly anti-racist one. As a merchant seaman he'd been around the world several times and had worked with people of all races. It's something he drummed into me all the time.' Livingstone was propelled closer to the Labour camp by the local Tory calls for repatriation of immigrants. He also became involved in trade unionism when he helped to organise a branch of ASTMS to oppose redundancies at the Chester Beatty research unit.

And so, at the age of twenty-three, Livingstone became motivated enough to join the local Norwood branch of the Labour Party. Although he had attended the odd anti-Vietnam war march and had subscribed for a year to an anarchist group called Solidarity, it was his first firm expression of political alignment.

He joined in 1968, just a couple of months before the spring riots in Paris, at a time when almost every other socialist of his age was deserting Labour for the headier comradeship of Trotskyism and other brands of insurrectionist politics.

'What I didn't realise when I joined the Labour Party was how totally debilitated it had become. I suppose 1968/9 must have been the absolute nadir in terms of active party membership. Half the people had actually resigned in protest about what Wilson was doing. They'd gone off to join other left-wing groups like IS [International Socialists] or just devoted themselves fully to trade unionism . . . I recognised that you weren't going to achieve social change other than through the Labour Party. No outside grouping was going to replace it . . .

'I joined thinking that there would be a really good chance in about ten years of getting on the local council if I worked really hard . . . By the time I went to my second branch meeting I was chairman and secretary of the Young Socialists and on the local government committee. By the time I went to the third, I was membership secretary of the party and on the executive committee. There was simply no one else around to do those sorts of things. Everybody else had left. It was incredible. At general management committee meetings in Norwood there were only about twenty-five people present . . .'

So Livingstone was ensconced in Norwood Labour politics before the left-wingers came streaming back from their various sects to give the local party the reputation for militancy which it still retains. In May 1971, he took his place for Labour on Lambeth council, the London borough of which Norwood forms part. (His father worked for him on polling day, but still voted Tory in a neighbouring ward.)

This timing was to be a crucial feature of Livingstone's political development. Although by that stage he had read widely, especially political biography, and had become fascinated by the study of voting behaviour, he had never undergone the rigorous ideological training through which contemporary recruits to Trotskyist parties and tendencies were passing. He had not studied the works of Karl Marx and, by the time he might have wanted to start, he was immersed in the minutiae of council agendas and the daily business of practical politics. Livingstone was, and still remains, ideologically untutored, more concerned with policies and the exercise of power than with theoretical analysis.

The issue which most concerned him at the time was Lambeth's serious housing problem and the failure of previous Labour councils to tackle it. 'During the 1960s Lambeth had been one of the real deadhead-type Labour boroughs,' he says. 'It had been run by a guy called Alderman Cotton. There were two or three competent but not very imaginative old working-class right-wingers, with about fifty lobby fodder supporters behind them, to run the whole show . . . Each year they would work out what the rate increase should be and then decide how many houses they could afford to build – perhaps two hundred in a good year. So Lambeth had a pretty mediocre housing programme.'

In the borough elections in 1968, when the Wilson government was at its most unpopular, the Conservatives won Lambeth from Labour with a huge majority of 57 seats to 3. The Tories had promised to cut the housing programme to reduce expenditure, but within a few weeks of taking office their leaders had a complete change of heart. 'The housing director, Harry Simpson, went to work on them and, by taking them round some of the most appalling deprived housing in Brixton where there was a black family to every room, really shook them rigid.' The result was that the Conservative administration quadrupled the housing programme left by Labour. 'So the whole of the Labour Party in Lambeth, having generally complained about the council for years, is horrified to see the Tories suddenly doing better, and dramatically so. The Tories set up a proper campaign against bad landlords and brought in multiple occupation controls. By 1970 the whole country is aware that the most dynamic housing area is Lambeth.'

The shame of being out-performed by the Tories encouraged younger members of the local Labour parties, on both left and right, to organise to clear out the council old guard during selection of candidates for the 1971 borough elections. When Labour won with a majority of 51 to 9, there was new blood, but by no means a left majority. Livingstone immediately became vice-chairman of housing, in charge of housing management. He is remembered for reforming council policy towards 'problem families' who had previously been corralled by housing department officials into three blocks of indescribable horror at the north end of the borough. The families were dispersed into better accommodation. He also persuaded the Labour group to make compulsory purchase orders on large numbers of private-rented properties by drawing attention to slum conditions and landlord racketeering. This covert municipalisation programme was to cause major difficulties for Lambeth's housing department, which never had the money to refurbish Livingstone's acquisitions.

In August 1973 he threatened to resign his vice-chairmanship if the council failed to honour promises to rehouse families from another three Dickensian half-way house council blocks, only slightly less appalling than the first three. He told the *South London Press*: 'Although I cannot give them a specific date, they have been let down in the past, so as a reassurance to make them feel better, I will resign if the council don't get moving this time.' The council did not get moving and after rows with the housing chairman on a range of issues, Livingstone resigned his office in December 1973. From then on he remained on the back benches until he left Lambeth council in 1978.

Although Livingstone was clearly at the radical end of the Lambeth Labour group, he was not in the early 1970s a fully-fledged left-winger. Ted Knight, who was later to become Labour leader of Lambeth council and one of Livingstone's closest political allies, remembers meeting him for the first time in 1970 and regarding him as a centrist member of the Labour Party: 'I viewed him as basically a [Harold] Wilson supporter, probably with some influence from people like [Tony] Crosland, if he was actually ever considering what Crosland was writing, which I doubt.' Knight himself had been expelled from the Labour Party in 1954 and had joined the Socialist Labour League, the Trotskyist forerunner of the Workers' Revolutionary Party. Knight worked for the SLL as an organiser before leaving them in the mid-1960s and being re-admitted into the Norwood branch of the

Labour Party in 1970. Under Knight's influence, Livingstone began to develop left-wing perspectives by a process of debate over issues rather than by any more theoretical schooling. Knight remembers that Livingstone initially supported British troops going into Northern Ireland and tended to 'see the good points' in the Tory Government's 1972 Housing Finance Act (which also enforced rent increases and led to the Clay Cross council rebellion). On both issues he changed his mind.

'I think it was quite useful for Ken to have somebody closely arguing with him who had very clearly defined views on matters of Labour Party and socialist policies, someone who had actually gone through the schools of Marxist training,' Knight observes. He believes that Livingstone learned from him a left-wing perspective on issues; and that he learned from Livingstone the value of building alliances across as broad a section of the left as possible. 'He was able to win wider support and was prepared to seek looser alliances than I would have been. That was his strength and my weakness; and that was why the team was a good one for the period,' says Knight.

Livingstone had opposed Knight when he stood for the chairmanship of the Norwood party in 1972, but by the end of that year they were starting to work together. They organised a purge to deselect all the Labour councillors representing Norwood who had not voted to defy the Housing Finance Act rent increases. (Livingstone's mind had changed in time for him to remain safely unpurged.)

So at the local elections in May 1974 Norwood returned a solid block of left-wingers who joined with a scattering of other leftists from other parts of the borough to form a disciplined group on the council, in conflict with the majority Labour administration. Knight and Livingstone jostled with each other for the leadership of the left minority and it is a moot point which of them would have emerged on top when the left took power in Lambeth after the 1978 local elections. But by then Livingstone had moved on to new struggles in a different part of London.

During the 1960s Livingstone had been living at home in Norwood with his parents. They had bought a cottage in Lincoln with the idea of retiring there, but in October 1971, just before they were ready to move, his father died of a heart attack. His mother stayed on in London for a year and, when she eventually moved up to Lincoln, Livingstone went into lodgings. For the first time, at the age of twenty-seven, he started living on his own.

While he had been working at the Chester Beatty research institute, he had gone to evening classes and gained another O-level in human anatomy, physiology and hygiene, and an A-level in zoology. This helped him move to another technician's job at the Sutton branch of the Royal Marsden hospital. But by 1970 he was becoming disillusioned with the work, which involved experiments with live animals. He says he began disagreeing more and more with the doctors about when experiments should be terminated and would often stop them without the doctors' agreement. It was the technician's responsibility to ensure that the animals did not suffer, but his frequent interventions caused considerable friction. 'At the same time I wanted to work with people rather than animals. Often it was a question of working for hours and hours on your own in a room in complete isolation. It was one of those units where you try and cut down the disease coming in. You had to step in troughs of disinfectant walking into the animal unit. The disinfectant was green. You'd end up with these brilliant green feet as it soaked through the canvas shoes you wore. People would occasionally see those feet and fall around in hysterics. They thought you had some rare disease you were being treated for.'

And so in 1970, after being out of school for eight years, with the scars of Tulse Hill School healed over, a green-footed Livingstone gained a place on a teacher training course at Philippa Fawcett College in south London. It was filled predominantly by young women from the Home Counties. 'I remember going to the first lecture. It was for the whole of the first year. The lecturer slowly built up to this climax: "A lot of you will deeply reject and resent what I am about to say and will feel that it is divisive and unpleasant. I ask you not to close your mind to it." He then went on to say that there is very strong evidence to suggest that there are different classes of people in society. There are working-class people and middle-class people. They have different perceptions of things. And the people in this audience gasped. I thought: my God, I've made a terrible mistake here.'

The course lasted three years and Livingstone says he probably had one of the worst attendance records. 'I got elected to Lambeth council at the end of my first year. I spent an awful lot of time at the council and very little time at the college. It was everything that was rotten with teacher training. You were told when you came that you would be assessed on your teaching practices in the third year, on twelve written bits of work and on the final exam which no one ever failed. There was a drop-out rate of perhaps five per cent of people having breakdowns and drug problems over the three years. Then, out of the two hundred people finally taking the exam, one would have a nervous breakdown during it, one would be drunk the night before and not turn up – and those were the only two who would fail. So you were told at the start that effectively, having got into the place, you were going to qualify. I did the twelve pieces of work that were required and not a stroke more and went and did the exam and got my qualification. But there was no pressure. It was a complete waste of three years . . .'

It was at teacher training college that he met his wife Christine. She was a year ahead of him and was president of the students' union when he was secretary. He left college in June 1973 and they married the following December. In May 1974 Christine joined Ken as a Lambeth Labour councillor.

At the time the borough council was still the main focus of Livingstone's political attention. But in May 1973 he had also won the election to be Norwood's representative on the GLC and ILEA. For anyone interested in housing the GLC then offered the best chance of solutions to Lambeth's problems. In 1973 there were 12,000 families on the Lambeth council housing waiting list and another 40,000 families living in property due for demolition within fifteen years. It seemed impossible to meet this public housing demand unless the GLC's resources of land and money from across London could be mobilised to do the job.

Ken and Christine made a joint decision that she would work as a teacher, allowing him to devote himself full-time to politics at

Lambeth and the GLC. 'We decided that I would do four years on the GLC and then see what happened at the end of it. Initially we thought I'd go back to teaching. But as my time at the GLC progressed I became more and more involved in it. Gradually the prospect of ever going into a teaching career faded away.' At the start Ken supplemented Christine's income with work for the local Labour Party. He was a paid deputy agent in the 1974 general elections. But the arrangement was only really made financially possible by one of the last decisions of Ted Heath's Conservative Government, to introduce an attendance allowance system for local councillors. 'When it started it was very good. In the first year it was about £2,000 or slightly more, which was the average national wage. They didn't increase it for about six years. So each year my income went down in real terms while Christine's went up as she got promotion ... I thought that, with the introduction of the attendance allowance system, you could actually have a full-time local government career. I thought I could achieve far more as a full-time local government politician than I could ever achieve as a backbench MP. All through that period from 1968 to 1975 I never tried to get selected as a Parliamentary candidate. I stayed fully active in local government. It wasn't until that period in 1975 when the government started to centralise a lot of decisions that I began to have ambitions in Parliament.

'Before then it seemed in local government that you had a chance actually to involve people in the running of their lives, to break up the concentrations of power – the theme you have heard me rabbit on about ever since. That was there for me from 1971. I realised you could do an awful lot with a borough council. As it was so much closer to the people, they could have more impact on it than anything to do with central government.'

This view was idiosyncratic at the time. Most activists on the left were concentrating their energies on the industrial side of the labour movement, on single-issue politics, or on the drive to increase accountability within the Labour Party which began with the formation of the Campaign for Labour Party Democracy in 1973. Livingstone virtually ignored these mainstream pursuits.

He spent his time moving between Lambeth council and the GLC, making trouble for their right-wing Labour leaders and organising for future victory by the left. In a memorable phrase, Lambeth councillor Elsie Horstead attacked him in 1976 for rubbishing the Lambeth leadership when he was at ILEA and rubbishing the ILEA leadership when he was at Lambeth. 'Here you have a waltzing mouse,' she said, 'who goes around from one group to another vilifying the other' (*South London Press*, 26.3.76).

In his early days on the GLC, however, Livingstone was not perceived by other members of the Labour group as being particularly left-wing. That recognition came when he took part in a revolt against spending cuts pushed through by the ruling Labour administration in 1975. This revolt and its subsequent consequences for the London Labour party formed the basis of the campaign which brought victory for the left in 1981. Before picking up this strand, it will be useful to see what it was that the GLC did and describe the old-guard Labour leaders against whom present political developments are a reaction.

3 · County Hall

The very existence of the GLC has always been controversial. It was set up by the London Government Act of 1963 as part of an effort to create a logical framework for administering the capital, which had long before developed from a city into a far-flung conurbation.

The origins of local government in London stretch back to Saxon times when the boundaries of the Square Mile of the City of London were established. The City Corporation, which appointed its first Mayor in 1192, resolutely refused over the centuries to extend its elitist jurisdiction to the urban area which grew up around it. As a result, most of London was governed until the end of the nineteenth century by scores of separate parishes, administered by 'vestries' elected by the ratepayers. This framework was unsuitable for the management of nineteenth-century social reforms such as the establishment of a police force, sewerage, paving, street lighting and a universal education service. So separate, indirectly elected boards were set up to manage these programmes of change, notably the Metropolitan Police Force (1829), the Metropolitan Board of Works (1855) and the London School Board (1870).

The first real effort to package these new municipal responsibilities into a proper democratic system came with the establishment of the London County Council in 1889. This was a directly elected body which covered the then urbanised parts of the traditional counties of Middlesex, Surrey and Kent. At the outset it had complete control of local services in this area. The Local Government Act of 1899 reduced its power by setting up a lower tier of twenty-eight metropolitan boroughs, but the LCC retained the leading role in the provision of public services, including housing and education.

This system worked pretty well through the early years of the

twentieth century, reaching its heyday in the Labour administrations of Herbert Morrison after 1934. Morrison consolidated
his position as a leading figure in the Labour Party through his
mastery of London's administrative machine. He lifted Labour's
morale after the Ramsay MacDonald crisis of 1931 by pushing
through major programmes of slum clearance and school building. And he demonstrated the power and independence of the
LCC when he refused to accept a Government veto on plans to
build a new Waterloo Bridge and completed the job by putting the
cost on the rates.

There were two reasons why the Conservative Government of
Harold Macmillan moved to get rid of the LCC. The first was that
its boundaries no longer reflected the further growth of the
London conurbation to cover all Middlesex and large swathes of
Surrey, Kent and Essex.

A Royal Commission on Local Government in Greater London, set up under Sir Edwin Herbert in 1957, concluded that a
single metropolitan authority was necessary to organise planning,
traffic management and highway construction over this wider
Greater London area. It also argued that the administration of
many services could best be passed to a lower tier of borough
councils which would be more closely in touch with the people
they served.

The logic of Herbert's arguments was sound, but it also
happened that they produced a second motive for reform by
providing a party political advantage for the Conservatives.
Whereas the old LCC boundaries ensured that London was
permanently Labour-controlled, the new wider London area
proposed by Herbert could almost be guaranteed to produce a
Conservative administration in County Hall.

For Labour, Morrison fulminated against the creation of a
GLC on the grounds that it would be far too large for efficient
administration. 'I will stump London and we will fight in London
to denounce the Government for this piece of political jobbery,' he
told the House of Lords in March 1962. It turned out, however,
that the GLC did not become such a bastion of Tory hegemony.
Nine true-blue Conservative districts on the fringes of the pro-

posed GLC area fought a successful rearguard action to stay outside it. Their leaders feared that their inclusion in London might quite lower the tone of their neighbourhoods and they believed (incorrectly) that it would add to the financial burden on their ratepayers.

Their departure left the GLC on a political knife-edge. It was won by Labour in 1964, Conservatives in 1967 and 1970, Labour in 1973, Conservatives in 1977 and Labour in 1981. Other changes were made to the Herbert proposals, notably the devolution of responsibility for education to the borough level (except in the original LCC area where an Inner London Education Authority of GLC and borough representatives was created to retain a unified education system in the centre). So, for the most part, administration was to be conducted on a smaller and more efficient scale than before. Few people now would argue that this decentralisation was wrong.

The 1963 London Government Act set up thirty-two borough councils, each with a minimum population size of 200,000, which were to become the main operational tier of local administration. They were made responsible for personal social services; refuse collection; environmental health services; most licensing functions; libraries and swimming baths; control of weights and measures, food and drugs, and noise and smoke control; consumer protection; registration of births, marriages and deaths; allotments; cemeteries; street cleansing; working conditions in shops and offices; and many other services. They also had first-level responsibility for a range of other functions which were split with the GLC, including housing, planning, roads and parks.

This left the GLC with the supposedly strategic functions, including planning for London as a whole; control of about 880 miles of the main metropolitan roads; traffic management; housing for the needs of London as a whole; refuse disposal; Thames flood prevention; land drainage; the fire brigade; and (until they were transferred to regional quangos in 1973) the ambulance and water services.

The carving up of responsibilities was never entirely satisfactory. The GLC was left with the appearance of power, inheriting

the splendid Edwardian classical edifice of County Hall on the
south bank of the Thames opposite the Houses of Parliament,
with its ornate marbled council chamber, seven miles of corridors
and 35,000 staff. It became the biggest council in Europe,
responsible for 610 square miles of territory and nearly 8 million
Londoners. But the GLC lacked sufficient strategic power to
pursue its proper role. It was sandwiched between boroughs
which resented its excessive interference in day-to-day matters of
planning and administration and a central government which
became increasingly reluctant to yield up truly strategic functions,
involving the control and distribution of resources. In spite of the
subsequent recommendations of the Marshall Inquiry on Greater
London in 1978, this contradiction has never been satisfactorily
resolved. (Nor is it likely to be by the proposals put forward by the
Thatcher government in 1983, which appear to solve the problem
by removing strategic control of London from the democratic
influence of Londoners.)

Even if the GLC was less than perfect, it was still worth fighting
for. Labour won the 1973 GLC election on a 10,000-word
manifesto called *A Socialist Strategy for London*. In many ways it was
a more ambitiously radical document than the one on which
Livingstone came to power in 1981. It was a final flowering of that
post-war optimism with which both Labour and Conservative
governments had encouraged local authorities to expand their
activities in pursuit of solutions to Britain's social problems.

The socialist strategy was prepared in 1972, three years before
Labour's Environment Secretary, Tony Crosland, told local government that 'the party's over' and the Chancellor, Denis Healey,
began to carve into its investment programmes. So, although the
manifesto was written by basically right-wing elements in the
London Labour Party establishment, it is still regarded with fond
nostalgia by the left. It proposed tackling London's acute housing
and transport problems through massive injections of additional
public spending.

There was no doubt that the problems were serious. The 1971
census had shown that 21 per cent of families in inner London
shared their homes with other families (compared with 4 per

The old order: Sir Reg Goodwin casts his vote (*Press Association*)

cent nationally; and that 37 per cent lacked exclusive use of a bath, hot water and a lavatory (compared with 18 per cent nationally).

Labour proposed a huge programme of public-sector house-building and the purchase of private landlords' property to bring it into council management. There was also a reaction against former bipartisan road-building plans for the capital, notably an inner motorway box, and a determination to revive public transport, using the GLC's new powers to control London Transport, for which it had assumed responsibility under the Transport (London) Act of 1969.

Labour promised to freeze London Transport fares as a first step towards their eventual abolition. It also pledged an improved pay and conditions package to LT staff to get rid of labour shortages which had created gaps in the service in spite of LT's efforts to recruit more staff from the West Indies.

Labour won the 1973 GLC election under the leadership of Sir Reg Goodwin, who, at the age of 64, was nearing the end of his career as general secretary of the National Association of Boys' Clubs. Goodwin had become Labour leader in 1967 after a devastating election defeat which reduced the Labour group to only eighteen members. He was the last of the political heirs of Herbert Morrison – men and women like Sir Isaac Hayward, Lord Fiske, Baroness Serota and Dame Evelyn Denington, who fitted comfortably into the nation's ruling establishment.

Goodwin was the GLC Labour member for Bermondsey, the inner-London constituency which became notorious in 1981/2 during Peter Tatchell's efforts to seize the Parliamentary nomination from its right-wing incumbent, Bob Mellish. But although Tatchell has harsh words to say about the Mellish constituency machine, he makes clear in his account of the affair (*The Battle for Bermondsey*, Heretic Books, 1983) that the left in Bermondsey felt no antagonism towards Goodwin: 'Despite political disagreements, we actually liked him.'

Goodwin was firmly committed to the 1973 GLC manifesto. Indeed he had written much of it himself. So when Labour was returned with a majority of 57 seats to 35, there was no disposition towards trimming or backsliding.

Leaders of the GLC have one great advantage over Prime Ministers. In Parliament most MPs of the governing party remain backbenchers, frustrated by their lack of office. At the GLC, such is the range of committees, sub-committees and special area boards, almost every majority party councillor can get a job. When Livingstone arrived as a new councillor, unknown to his elders and betters, they made him vice-chairman of what was popularly called the filthy films panel – the Film Viewing Board which still in those days viewed films to check their suitability for the London public. Within a year he became deputy chairman of housing management.

For a while he and his colleagues proceeded in relative harmony to implement their manifesto promises. Fares were frozen and the first London-wide system of concessionary fares for pensioners was quickly introduced. Although by then LT was no longer experiencing serious staff shortages, an £80 million programme of pay and conditions improvements was introduced without extracting productivity concessions. Gladys Dimson, as chairwoman of housing development, started municipalising large tracts of London and acquiring land for the enhanced building pro-gramme. In February 1974, Labour's first budget increased the rates by 46 per cent from 6.6p to 9.5p in the pound. As the Conservative opposition was quick to point out, this was really equivalent to an 85 per cent increase after allowing for the fact that ambulance and water responsibilities had been removed from the GLC with the setting up of regional water and health authorities in 1973.

The Goodwin administration, however, rapidly moved into a financial crisis. This was the period when the annual rate of inflation began to spiral almost out of control, reaching a peak of 26 per cent in July 1975. Such unprecedented pressure on pay and prices played havoc with the GLC's current expenditure budget. The most serious damage was caused by the impact of rising interest rates on a GLC debt of around £1.6 billion. Most of this was long-term money borrowed years before to build houses,

Livingstone on the march, April 1, 1973. The occasion was a protest against GLC proposals to enclose the Crystal Palace lakes and monsters and charge admission (*Patrick Smith Associates*)

roads and the like, when rates of interest were only 3 or 4 per cent; but as these loans matured the money was having to be re-borrowed at 12 or 13 per cent.

Inflation also dramatically increased the cost of the fares freeze commitment. London Transport, which had balanced its books from 1969 to 1973, was by the autumn of 1974 warning of an impending deficit of £120 million because of its inability to recoup the cost of pay settlements through higher fares.

If Labour had gone ahead with its full manifesto programme the GLC rate in April 1975 would have had to be about 22½p in the pound – an increase of 137 per cent when the Labour government was pleading for rate rises to be held down to 25 per cent. Further big increases would have been required in the run-up to the next GLC elections in 1977.

This was only part of Goodwin's problem. The manifesto programme, coming on top of the large inherited loan debt, made massive demands on the GLC's capacity to borrow. In early 1975 Maurice Stonefrost, its Comptroller of Finance, had a series of secret meetings with the Government and top City financiers in an effort to maintain the council's financial credibility. There was no danger that London might have followed the pattern of New York, which in that year narrowly avoided bankruptcy when it could no longer continue borrowing to pay its employees' wages. In England it is illegal for councils to borrow to finance such current expenditure; they may only take out loans for capital investment projects which are then paid off over subsequent years.

Stonefrost realised, however, that the stream of borrowing commitments which would arise over the following three to five years could not be satisfied by the money markets. Under the rules then in force, the Government approved the GLC's capital investment programme without taking any responsibility for ensuring that it could actually be financed. It gave the GLC a limited access to borrowing from the Government through the Public Works Loan Board; above the limit the council had to go out to the commercial sector. Stonefrost's researches showed that there could be no hope that the markets would agree to finance the GLC's likely demands. The financial name of London was at risk.

He finally convinced the Government of the need to open up an additional line of credit from the PWLB which would enable the council to finance its authorised programme – albeit at somewhat higher interest rates. This averted a crisis. Yet Stonefrost remained desperately concerned about the Labour administration's commitment to increase borrowing to finance its burgeoning housebuilding and municipalisation programme. About a year before the Labour government, under pressure from the International Monetary Fund, forced councils to cut their capital programmes, Stonefrost was warning the politicians to prepare to draw in their horns.

These pressures on the rates and on borrowing might by now have been consigned to an obscure footnote of GLC financial history if it had not been for the political ructions they caused. As the financial crisis developed through 1974 and early 1975, the Goodwin administration felt itself obliged to make a series of cuts which are now regarded in the folklore of the London Labour left as a gross act of betrayal.

From the perspective of the left, the process of backsliding began in May 1974 when leading committee chairmen went to a hotel at Aldermaston for a weekend of discussions with the GLC's chief officers. There was nothing novel about such an expedition. GLC officials say that it was merely a more spartan version of the weekend sessions they had held with the previous Conservative administration under Sir Desmond Plummer in the plusher surroundings of the Chewton Glen conference centre in the New Forest. The purpose, they say, was to enable the politicians to give officers a sense of direction about where the council was moving. To the left, however, it appeared that the process of education was the other way around.

Livingstone now recalls: 'Goodwin and the others all came back from Aldermaston committed to the idea of ending the massive fares subsidy . . . The argument was that if we carried on subsidising fares at this rate we would have to increase rents or cut the house-building programme, because otherwise the rate burden would be too enormous.' Goodwin's proposals were rejected by the Labour group in May 1974 on the grounds that it would be political folly to raise fares ahead of the expected October general election. The leadership resubmitted the plan a few weeks later. 'They claimed that London Transport had produced new financial projections which were even worse than before,' says Livingstone. 'I managed to block that by arguing it was a rescinding motion which needed a two-thirds majority. By that time they had the votes for a simple majority but not two-thirds . . . There were incredible speeches. I was accused of intimidating the group. It was the first time there was a real wave of hatred in my direction.'

So the fares, for a while, stayed down. Then, with the October general election out of the way, Goodwin's lieutenants got down to the job of vigorously lobbying group support for a 36 per cent fare increase for the following spring. 'Everyone was told that if it didn't go through Goodwin was going to resign and the administration would collapse. We ended up with a total crushing of the left.' The necessary votes were put through without discussion and the package was announced by Goodwin on October 31.

'The argument advanced for fare increases was still that they were necessary to save the house-building programme and rent levels. But after a few more weeks had passed, they came back and said there had to be a rent increase too (adding 50p a week to average GLC rent levels of £4.90) . . . We picked up quite a respectable vote against that one in group because people felt they were really being messed about.'

These increased charges helped to keep the GLC rate rise announced in February 1975 down to 80 per cent (nine-tenths of it attributable to inflation). By April, however, Goodwin came back to the group with proposals for £50 million cuts in the housing investment programme. This was the period when Tony Crosland, as Environment Secretary, was fighting in Cabinet against the Treasury's demands for public expenditure cuts. His political adviser, David Lipsey, rang round selected members of the GLC Labour group pleading with them to stick to the existing programme in support of Crosland's economic stance in the Cabinet debate.

These conflicting signals threw the Labour group into confusion. Two prominent members on the right, Dr Stephen Haseler and Douglas Eden (both of whom were later active in getting the Social Democrat bandwagon moving) made an abortive attempt to depose Goodwin. They argued that he had done too little too late to raise fares and rents to save the housing investment programme.

Livingstone and the left argued fiercely against every kind of cut. But Goodwin beat off the challenge from both wings and, on April 30, the housing cuts were carried through the group. In a memorandum to the meeting, Goodwin explained: 'It should be borne in mind that these cuts are necessary because of the rising cost of servicing capital debts, and if they are not made now more severe cuts will need to be made in election year 1976/7. Cuts now would mean greater room for manoeuvre and less of a rate increase in the run-up to the GLC elections. This could mean the difference between a Labour win in 1977 with a modified housing programme or Labour losing with a higher but unacceptably expensive housing programme.'

Five members of the administration were sacked or resigned their posts: Haseler (chairman of the general purposes committee) and Eden (vice-chairman of housing development), representing the right; Livingstone (vice-chairman of housing management) and David White (chairman of the southern area planning board), representing the left; and Gladys Dimson (chairwoman of housing development), representing neither left nor right, but a passionate supporter of the housing programme for which she had been responsible.

Goodwin admitted to the *Sunday Times* (18.5.75) that Labour's manifesto, written in 1972, now seemed to have been conceived in 'virtually a different era' – in other words that it had been overtaken by the dictates of hard financial logic. He never earned the intended benefit of sacrificing his promises. Although the GLC rate was held steady in February 1976 and 1977 he crashed to a 64 seats to 28 defeat in the 1977 GLC elections.

The story of the Goodwin leadership is essential background for understanding the Livingstone administration of 1981. Reaction against the cuts provided a focus for the mobilisation of the left. Reaction against Goodwin's non-participative style of leadership provided the motivation for the older-guard members of the centre to support the left when it came to a choice between Livingstone and McIntosh for leader.

Leading characters in the Goodwin administration included Illtyd Harrington, the deputy leader and finance chairman who was responsible for pushing through the cuts, and Harvey Hinds, the chief whip who organised a majority for them. Both went on to support Livingstone in 1981 and become senior figures in his administration.

The public revolt of the left against the Goodwin cuts started at the council meeting on June 10. Nine Labour councillors issued a statement condemning measures 'which are diametrically opposed to the election manifesto on which we were elected in April 1973'. Livingstone, Tony Banks, David White, Dudley Barker, Marie Jenkins, Maureen Harwood, Frank Archer, David Chalkeley and Dick Collins announced: 'We will not be supporting these measures either in the council chamber or outside of it in the party at large.' In particular they condemned the investment cuts in which 'housing has been singled out for the most destructive attack since before the last war'. They also criticised fare and rent increases as 'an attack on the living standards of ordinary Londoners for the benefit of the large commercial ratepayers of the City'. The 50p a week rent increase would save the average domestic ratepayer a mere 1p a week and the 25 per cent fare increase only 9p per week, they said: 'It seems to us to be a total rejection of the social contract to implement policies of this nature at a time when trades unionists are being pushed by the government to take wage increases which do not keep pace with price increases.' The statement called on the Government to end the GLC's crippling debt charges 'as part of an overall socialist economic strategy to solve present economic problems'.

The rebels formed a campaign called Labour Against Housing Cuts to fight their case through the party. Its inaugural conference in July 1975 established three main demands: that councils should be given powers to requisition all empty property; that there should be no cuts in investment in public housing; and that the GLC and Government must return to the policy of the manifestos on which they were elected. The campaign never tried to mobilise mass support and it involved no more than about fifty activists in a series of open-door meetings (LAHC records show that its opening conference was attended by two Labour MPs who later joined the SDP). But it provided the rudiments of a political network and organisation for getting policies accepted by the London Labour Party conference and running a slate of candidates for the regional executive.

Livingstone was initially working on the assumption that Labour might win the GLC elections in 1977. The Labour government, which had come to power in 1974 with a majority of only three, seemed unlikely to survive by-election defeats. 'We could easily have seen the election of a Thatcher administration in late 1975 or 1976,' says Livingstone. 'And in that case we could have looked forward to holding control of the GLC.' (Government parties tend to do badly in mid-term local elections.)

Livingstone's priorities therefore were to get the London Labour Party conference to condemn the Goodwin cuts, to prepare an acceptable manifesto for the 1977 elections and to ensure that left-wingers would have a majority on the new GLC Labour group.

His campaign, however, had only limited success. Resolutions attacking the cuts and establishing mandatory reselection for GLC candidates were passed by the conference in March 1976. But the left failed to make any ground in elections for the regional executive in that year. As a result Goodwin was able to push through what Livingstone regarded as an 'appalling' GLC manifesto which he and others publicly condemned as 'anti-party' on the day before its publication. The left subsequently won control of the regional executive in March 1977 (the month when the Lib-Lab Pact allowed the Labour Government to prolong its hold on office in return for the abandonment of socialist measures).

By mid-1976 Livingstone had given up hopes that Labour could win the 1977 GLC elections, which showed every sign of becoming a Tory landslide. 'I decided, after discussing it with my local party, that I should try to find a safe seat. We needed to have a left-wing element in the rump to organise and pull it together for the next election four years later.'

So Livingstone switched from Norwood to Hackney North, where he succeeded the retiring GLC chairman, Lord Pitt. He told the *South London Press*: 'You cannot just have a socialist revolution in Norwood and nowhere else.'

Livingstone selected as prospective Labour Parliamentary Candidate for Hampstead, June 1977 (*Canton Studios*)

This was the first of Livingstone's frequent changes of constituency, which came to earn him a reputation as a carpetbagger . In GLC and Parliamentary elections he has never gone for the same seat twice. But his reasoning at the time was sound. 'I was the only one of the old Labour lefties to survive.'

The 1977 defeat was Labour's worst GLC result since 1967. On both occasions the mid-term unpopularity of a Labour government was more to blame than anything to do with GLC administration. Even if Labour had won, insufficient left-wingers had been selected to produce a left GLC. In that sense Livingstone's campaign had failed.

So, as Cutler's Conservative administration got down to the job of slimming down the GLC, the attentions of the left switched away from County Hall to prepare for the next Parliamentary election. Livingstone's ideas for a left-led GLC were put on ice while he got down to the serious business of trying to become an MP.

A month after Labour's GLC defeat, Livingstone narrowly won selection as the party's prospective Parliamentary candidate for Hampstead. He and Christine moved house to live in the constituency, arriving just in time for him to qualify for election to Camden borough council which he joined in May 1978.

He was already by then becoming known to readers of the local paper, the *Hampstead and Highgate Express*. In August 1977 he had been made to pay £250 in costs after bringing an unsuccessful legal action against a Department of the Environment planning inspector, holding a public inquiry into proposals for a motorway at nearby Archway. Livingstone claimed the inspector had hit him in the mouth; the magistrate concluded that although it was possible that the inspector's hand had come in contact with Livingstone's face, there was no proof that it was done aggressively.

In September 1977 Livingstone caused more controversy by promising that if he were elected to Parliament he would do all he could to get the age of consent for homosexual men reduced from twenty-one to sixteen. And in March 1978 he launched a blistering attack on Camden council's Labour leadership: 'I have been to group meetings and I was shocked at the way they are run. The leadership try to rush things through and stop backbench councillors from raising important matters,' he told the *Ham and High* reporter. 'Some members even have to raise issues in the council chamber in the hope of inducing the Tories to side with them because they couldn't even discuss it with their own group. It's near-anarchy.' This is not the sort of thing new candidates for a council usually say less than two months before the elections.

In spite of these warning signals, Camden council was not prepared for Livingstone's impact on arrival. He won a surprise victory in a contest to become chairman of housing – largely because he persuaded the group to allow the candidates to make speeches and as usual made a good one. The *Ham and High* reported on May 26: 'Mr Livingstone has followed up his capture of the plum post by announcing a whirlwind of controversial policies which he hopes will bring radical changes in the council's Housing Department from top to bottom.' At the first meeting of the new housing committee in June, Livingstone 'amazed his colleagues and opposition alike by abandoning the usual staid formality of council meetings, accepting comments and discussion from the public and committing the council very much more to the principle of tenant consultation. And his almost presidential-style handling of the meeting underscored his reputation as an uncompromising left-winger.'

When the public part of the agenda finally ended after four and a half hours of lively debate, the committee had decided to freeze rents for a year, reform the system of rate collection, slash rents on houses undergoing repairs, change rent arrears procedures and put through some compulsory purchase orders (following personal representations at the meeting by a tenant). The Conservative leader, Alan Greengross (who was later to become Livingstone's opponent as leader of the GLC Conservatives), commented: 'Mr Livingstone is very keen to be a new broom – and heaven knows we need a new broom in the Housing Department – but it may be that he has brought along the wrong broom entirely' (*Ham and High*, 30.6.78).

Whether it was the right broom or the wrong broom, it was the broom which Livingstone had been busy fashioning on the backbenches on Lambeth council. He recalls: 'I knew exactly what I wanted to do because I'd been criticising everybody else for not doing it in Lambeth borough for the previous seven years.' He took the unprecendented step of setting up his own office inside the Housing Department and dealing directly with its middle management, bypassing the housing director except for once-a-week meetings. When officers failed to produce a report on time, he wrote his own on a couple of sides of paper and pushed it through committee. Grandiose building schemes were abandoned and resources channelled into modernising existing council homes and bringing large numbers of private properties into municipal ownership. Homes were let on short-term contracts with squatting organisations, fuelling allegations that Livingstone was deliberately bringing left-wing activist supporters into the

borough and on to the electoral register. In October 1978 Livingstone lost a censure motion in Camden council when five Labour
members refused to support him against Tory allegations that he
was housing single homeless squatters in preference to people on
its waiting list. He said they had got their facts wrong and refused
to resign.

Gerry Isaaman, editor of the *Ham and High*, says: 'What we first
noticed about him was that here was a man who could, unplanned,
get up in the council chamber and wipe the floor with the
opposition. He wowed them.'

But his style of administering housing inevitably led to chaos.
Livingstone would promise everyone that he would solve their
personal problems with every intention of doing so, says Isaaman.
'He gave tenants his home phone number and would get calls in
the middle of the night. He tried to play the role of the magician
. . . So he created around himself a mound of work so big that no
one in the world could cope with it. Camden's housing was always
in a mess, but he significantly increased the logjam.'

Roy Shaw, Labour leader of Camden council at the time, is less
charitable. 'He was a lousy chairman of housing,' he says. 'He was
totally in the pocket of the officers . . . His main concern was using
the position as a platform to get publicity for himself . . . Housing
committees were an absolute bear garden.' Shaw says that after
Livingstone left the job, his successor realised within three
months that the department needed a complete management
overhaul. 'Ken was prepared to accept the old position. He gets
bored with administration. He doesn't like detail.' It is a charge
which was to arise again when Livingstone took power at the
GLC.

But Shaw, twenty years Livingstone's senior and part of the
older Tribunite left of the Party, has more serious allegations
about Livingstone's behaviour. 'One of his tricks when he was on
Camden council was that he played to the gallery: the left-wing
gallery, the trades union gallery, whatever gallery would help him
at any particular moment. His ploy was to put forward an outrageous proposition, knowing full well that it would not be
accepted – not really believing it himself. It would be defeated in

the [Labour] group. He could then turn round and say: it's all the fault of those right-wing bastards; if it had been left to me, I would have done so and so. Thus he became the hero of a trades union group or whatever group he was particularly interested in at that moment. He did this on several occasions. Sometimes he did it so blatantly that, in speaking to the motion, he would say: I fully appreciate that there may well be members here who cannot support this motion, people who own their own homes, with families, who can't risk surcharge [a fine on councillors for unreasonable spending]. He was more or less saying: for heavens sake don't vote for this. And of course it would be defeated. Now there was one occasion when he did this and something went seriously wrong.'

In February 1979, during the so-called winter of discontent which defeated the Callaghan government's claim to have a workable incomes policy, Livingstone proposed a local settlement with the council's NUPE employees who were engaged on a national strike for better pay. He won the support of the Labour group for offering a £60 minimum wage which turned out to be much more generous than NUPE's eventual national agreement. Extra payments of up to £12.65 a week for the council's lowest-paid employees became known as the 'Camden supplement'. The district auditor later took the Labour councillors to court alleging that the supplement was 'unreasonable' spending and illegal. The case became a major test of the scope of local authorities' discretion.

Shaw claims that Livingstone never expected the Labour group to agree to pay the Camden supplement and that it was simply one more of his tactical demands to discredit the leadership. Livingstone says he was genuinely keen to settle the strike, not least to help council tenants who were on the phone to him complaining that their heating had been cut off. 'It wasn't an unreasonable demand. You would probably have voted for it yourself. You would have been embarrassed that you were employing people in their forties and fifties on £35 a week, given what you were earning. That was, I think, why I won in the end in the group. A lot of its middle-class members, who were earning £10,000, £15,000 or £20,000 a year, were horrified to discover that a lot of our workforce were taking home not much more than they were giving their kids for pocket money.'

The district auditor's case eventually came before the High Court in 1982 when the judges ruled that the Labour councillors had not acted unreasonably. If the case had gone the other way, they could all have been bankrupted. Councillors who vote to spend money unlawfully can be personally surcharged for the full amount. In the case of the Camden supplement, this sum was more than £1 million.

With this threat hanging over the Labour councillors, it became much harder for Livingstone to win majorities within the group by virtue of his sheer ability to win an argument. When his two-year term as housing chairman was over, he did not get the alternative front-bench post he was looking for. Shaw comments: 'For the last two and a half years anything Ken proposed would almost automatically be turned down because people saw through him. You will find that that has happened almost everywhere he has been.' Livingstone claims he would have succeeded to the leadership of Camden if he had still been there when the left swept into power after the local elections in May 1982. But (if readers will forgive a phrase which is becoming rather familiar) by then he had moved on to new struggles in different parts of London.

Livingstone had not come to Camden primarily to take over its council. He fully expected to become the Labour MP for Hampstead at the general election which was eventually declared in May 1979. His alliances in the run-up to this campaign provide further evidence of Livingstone's willingness to work with (but not to join) groupings on the fringes of the Labour movement.

In July 1978 he became a founder member of the Socialist Campaign for Labour Victory, an amalgam of several left groups operating in London at the time. It was his participation in this organisation which earned him the reputation as a Trotskyist fellow-traveller which he has not made any real effort to shake off. So it is important to establish what he and it were about.

The objective of SCLV was set out clearly in an editorial in the first issue (October 1978) of its newspaper, *Socialist Organiser*:

The SCLV aims for a massive Labour vote, but a vote with a difference. We want to keep the Tories out, but to do so campaigning for socialist policies and against the pro-capitalist 'record' of the Labour Government, which has consistently bitten the hands that voted it into office in 1974 . . . The SCLV will draw its life blood from the militants involved in the struggles over the past few years, by women, immigrants, youth and workers fighting the wage curbs. We take inspiration from struggles like the Grunwick workers', the fightback by Asian youth (and white working-class youth in the Anti-Nazi League) against racism and fascism, and the women of Trico who battled for equal pay. Together with these new militants we can re-invigorate the Labour movement, shake it up, and radically re-arm and organise it for struggle against capitalism . . . Our campaign must make sure that the Tories are combated, and that the newly-elected Labour Government, from its first days, faces a vocal socialist left-wing, vigorously demanding it cuts its slavish ties to the bankers and the bosses, and prepared to struggle against the Government every time it sells out.

The language of this editorial gives some clues to SCLV's parentage. It drew together many of the left groups on the outer fringes of the Labour Party, with the exception of Militant. Supporters of Workers Action and the Chartists played a leading role. Livingstone says he recognises that he and Ted Knight, who had recently become leader of Lambeth council, were brought in to give SCLV 'a degree of credibility with the completely un-aligned left' which always outnumbered members of organised groups within the Labour Party. To that extent he acknowledges he was being used. But Livingstone maintains that he was never personally involved in the business of sectarian politics. His objective and style of operation were to mobilise alliances on the left to fight specific campaigns on as broad a front as possible.

Livingstone is disparaging of the post-war British left's capacity to fragment itself in theological disputes over arcane points of principle. Once upon a time in the 1940s there was a relatively clear division between the (pro-Moscow) Communist Party and the (Trotskyist) Revolutionary Communist Party. The RCP broke up in the 1950s to form three main strands around Gerry Healy (Socialist Labour League/Workers Revolutionary Party), Tony Cliff (International Socialists/Socialist Workers Party) and Ted

Grant (Militant Tendency). These three groupings have themselves divided over time into further grouplets. As Livingstone
puts it: 'From that point on you just had a series of splits,
occasionally around obscure points of doctrine, like whether or
not we should consider that Russia is a state capitalist nation or a
deformed workers' state. Then, overlying that, you have massive
personality clashes . . . Everybody who's been around for a while
on the left has been moving backwards and forwards across an
increasingly larger number of split-off groups, expelling and
condemning each other from those groups, for twenty-five years.
So there are the most virulent personality clashes . . .

'I fortunately became politically active after most of this lot had
left the [Labour] Party. I just always operated within the Labour
Party and was prepared to work with any left groupings inside it or
outside it on a series of policy issues.

'So what tends to happen with me is that for a couple of years I
get on very well with several groupings on the left; then one of
them will fall out with me and condemn me for a couple of years.
Then they come back when they want me to do something. The
relationship goes hot and cold. I just never get involved in the
sectarian infighting between them.'

Livingstone's own campaign to win the seat in Hampstead
secured a comparatively good result in a bad Labour year. The
sitting MP, Geoffrey Finsberg, doubled the Conservative majority
to 3,681, but the swing to the Tories in Hampstead was only 2.1
per cent, compared with a national average of 5.2 per cent and an
inner London average of 7.1 per cent. Swings to the Tories in the
neighbouring borough of Hackney (averaging 10.3 per cent) and
Islington (9.3 per cent) and in the other Camden seats of Holborn
and St Pancras South (8.1 per cent) and St Pancras North (5.4 per
cent) suggest that the Hampstead electorate at least were not put
off by Livingstone's left-wing credentials. He got 315 more votes
than Labour had scored in 1974. Since Michael Foot was a
Hampstead elector, it can be assumed that the future Labour
leader supported him then (probably for the first and last time).

4 · Briefing

Even before his defeat at Hampstead, Livingstone had begun work to prepare for the next battle. By March 1979 his attention had reverted to the GLC. Writing in the SCLV paper, *Socialist Organiser*, he complained: 'The left . . . are giving no thought to the impending GLC election. Already the right have started to organise to revive the discredited old guard who were responsible for the disgusting record of the last Labour GLC between 1973 and 1977 . . . Those who have a commitment to a socialist GLC need to start organising now if this motley crew are to be prevented from discrediting the Labour Party in the eyes of the electorate for the second time in a decade.'

The article explained changes in the London Labour Party rules which ensured that the manifesto would be prepared by a regional party conference and not by the GLC leadership. It set out the timetable for mandatory reselection of candidates. And it argued: 'The candidates who are selected must be bound by the manifesto, which must give a clear lead in the direction of a fare-free system for public transport and a massive expansion in the housing programme under an expanded direct labour organisation.'

Livingstone concluded: 'There is now a desperate need for a London-wide left caucus of those interested in the GLC and local councils so that we can compare and discuss what is happening in each borough.' *London Labour Briefing* was under way.

Livingstone's interest in the GLC was at the time regarded by most of his comrades as idiosyncratic, not to say a little batty. It was all very well for him to launch attacks on the right-wing leadership (such as his tirade against £17 million cuts made by ILEA in the *Socialist Organiser* of October 1979). But few people on the left regarded the GLC as worth much attention, let alone the time and trouble of getting elected to it. Livingstone was at that stage advancing very conventional arguments about what it could do. He acknowledges that he had not thought out the policies of job creation and grants which were to take the 1981 administration into pioneering socialist territory. Nor had he fully realised the GLC's potential as a publicity platform. 'In the immediate period just before and just after the 1979 election, my thoughts were much more orthodox, basically along the lines of public transport and a decent housing programme.'

What Livingstone did, however, was to convince a lot of people on the left that the GLC election was the next battle on the agenda. It is this record on which his reputation as a formidable political organiser has come to be based.

'I remember going round the Labour Party conference in Brighton in October 1979 to just about everyone who lived in London and was on the left, saying: you really have got to think about standing for the GLC. October 1979 to May 1980 was the critical period to persuade left-wingers to come on the panel of candidates . . . I did the work on my own. There wasn't anyone else then. Nobody had paid much attention to the GLC.'

After the conference, Livingstone immediately called a meeting of the London left to discuss how it should organise to take over the council. This drew a furious response from John Keys, the right-wing general secretary of the London Labour Party. He claimed that Livingstone, as a member of the regional executive committee (EC), was abusing its 'very special role' in supervising the manifesto and candidate selection process. In a letter to EC members, Keys wrote: 'It is wrong for members of the EC to in any way undermine the impartial responsibility of the EC by participating in factional meetings which could undermine the integrity of the Regional EC . . . I hope the EC will ensure that its insistence on fairness and merit and refraining from trying to influence GMCs [local constituency parties] will continue.'

Livingstone, however, did not back down. He christened the meeting on October 18 the 'John Keys Annual Memorial Lecture' and used it to begin the process of educating the London left in the procedures for drawing up the manifesto and becoming candidates.

LONDON LABOUR BRIEFING

10p   TRIAL ISSUE

TAKING OVER THE G.L.C.

LABOUR MUST WIN IN 1981

by Ken Livingstone
(Hackney North GLC member)

1980 is the year in which we will determine policy and select the candidates for the May 1981 GLC election. For the first time the election will be a major event in the struggle against a Tory government.

By the end of this year the government plan to have passed legislation forcing the sale of council houses and giving Heseltine power to withhold government funds from councils refusing to make cuts.

Undoubtedly the Tories will try to use those new powers and select several London Labour boroughs as the prime targets in their campaign.

The election must be used to rally support for councils refusing to make cuts and to mobilise opposition to the Tories' policies. It will be a major defeat for the Tories if we win a decisive majority on the GLC at the height of Heseltine's attack on Labour councils.

GLC and ILEA finances must be used to help any Labour borough from whom Heseltine withholds government finance.

An immediate decision to close down the GLC Housing Disposals department will stiffen the resolve of borough councils to refuse to sell council housing.

It is this role into which the GLC will be thrust which is responsible for the present interest in GLC election plans — in marked contrast to the past. At previous elections few have been willing to stand due to daytime meetings and the remoteness of the GLC — most activists have directed their attention to the borough councils. This has led to the GLC/ILEA Labour groups being even less representative than the Parliamentary Labour Party. Now there is something close to hysteria amongst these people as for the first time in many years they face a serious challenge to their positions.

Already a third of the Labour group have decided to retire and others are becoming regular attenders at their GMCs for the first time since the last elections.

Three recent decisions by the Greater London Labour Party have disturbed the present Labour group.

1. The London annual meeting has voted in favour of automatic reselection for all GLC members thus ensuring the first selection meeting in living memory in some constituencies.

2. The Regional Executive has decided that the GLC election manifesto shall be determined by the whole party at a full delegate meeting on the 18th of October.

In the past the manifesto was written by a small group (including a full time GLC officer!) and steamrolled through the Regional Executive with threats of resignation if any major changes were made.

This year the Regional Executive will circulate discussion documents to all affiliated organisations and these will be

(cont. on bottom page two)

Editorial:

This is the first trial edition of *London Labour Briefing*. Your initial reaction may be that the left needs another newspaper like it needs another Reg Prentice. However, this is a bulletin with a difference. It is not produced or controlled by any one tendency or group, and does not claim to be able to provide full coverage of international events or to give an in depth theoretical analysis on every issue! We have set ourselves the more modest but vital task of keeping active militants inside the Labour Party and the unions in London in touch with each other and up to date on what is happening in the various battles across the capital.

No doubt you yourself have often been misled or confused by stories about events in neighbouring Boroughs and in other CLPs. If we can lift some of the fog that surrounds us so often we will be achieving part of our job.

Comrades should also be aware that this year we begin the arduous task of selecting our candidates for the GLC elections in 1981. For far too long the largest local authority in Western Europe has been the 'poor relation' as far as Labour Party organising and activity is concerned. We aim to rectify this by giving full coverage to the many issues involved: housing, transport, education and finance amongst them. We will also cover the various selections and candidates as the need arises.

Perhaps even more important are the Borough elections for the following year. We will systematically cover each borough borough's record, what its Labour councillors have done and the issues locally that affect the Labour movement. We will also follow the new re-selection procedures for parliamentary candidates and sitting MPs, which we strongly support as a means of making our elected representatives more accountable. We will also cover the activities of bodies like the GLRC, GLATCs and the South East Region of the TUC.

If this venture is to succeed we need your help: not in a passive sense of reading and donating to us (though that certainly helps) but as active contributors. If this is to give comprehensive coverage we need input from every Borough in London. If you are willing to be a 'keyperson' for your CLP or area, please write to us and attend the various meetings we organise.

We are now at a crucial time for Labour. If a successful fight is to be mounted against the cuts, and if this Tory Government is to be removed, then we must prepare now for the enormous struggles ahead. Organisation and information are the keys to success. Make sure you become an effective component of our overall strength. One contribution towards this will be *your* support for this new publication.

By this stage the regional executive was firmly in the hands of a broad hard and soft left alliance; but the left had already pushed through changes in the rules to ensure that control over the manifesto and candidacies was passed to the grassroots level. London is such a large conurbation that there is little contact between its far-flung constituencies. So to win the GLC for the left, it was necessary to build up political networks to stimulate and co-ordinate local activity. Livingstone organised a series of meetings at rooms he had booked in County Hall to promote discussion on policy areas, such as housing and industry policy. He also sent out a stream of letters to individuals whose names and addresses he kept on a card-index file of the London left (which must be the most comprehensive outside the Special Branch). These passed on information about selection procedures. 'I sent all the people on the left a list of all the constituencies in order of winnability, with a note about who the present member was, whether they were standing down, what the address of the party secretary was, how to get where they were in London – a sort of guide to how to get selected.'

A typical example was a photocopied handwritten note on May 1, 1980: 'Dear Comrade, I enclose information re the GLC seats in London which we can expect to win in next year's elections. Please write immediately to those which you would like to contest with brief statements of biographical details and political views. Send several copies to each CLP [constituency] secretary for ease of circulation to ward branch meetings. Many seats have now started the selection process, so it is essential to write immediately.'

On August 22, he wrote again: 'Whilst most of the safe Labour seats have selected, most of the marginal seats we need to win from the Tories are still looking for candidates . . . I get constant phone calls from these constituencies asking if there is "anyone left on the panel worth selecting", so do please write to them with a brief statement of your political views. Yours fraternally, Ken Livingstone.'

This emphasis on the marginals was an important factor in building the eventual victory of the left. It would be misleading to suggest that Livingstone singlehandedly organised the selection process across London. Many of the left candidates who eventually became councillors would deny that he had anything to do with their decision to stand or with their success in getting selected. But his efforts contrasted sharply with the almost total lack of London-wide planning by the right wing.

Another key development was the founding of a new left periodical called *London Labour Briefing*. In late 1979 the Socialist Campaign for Labour Victory had been taken over by a hard-line faction which argued that councils should advance the class struggle by refusing to make any cuts in services or to put up the rates. (This faction subsequently became known by the title of its newspaper, *Socialist Organiser*.)

Livingstone and a number of other SCLV activists, including Chartists and independent left-wingers, therefore quit SCLV to set up a new grouping around the campaign to win the GLC for the left. In February 1980 they brought out the first 'Trial Issue' of *London Labour Briefing*, which told readers in an editorial:

Your initial reaction may be that the left needs another newspaper like it needs another Reg Prentice. However, this is a bulletin with a difference. It is not produced by any one tendency or group, and does not claim to be able to provide full coverage of international events or to give an in-depth theoretical analysis on every issue! We have set ourselves the more modest but vital task of keeping active militants inside the Labour Party and the unions in London in touch with each other and up to date on what is happening in the various battles across the capital.

A lead story written by Livingstone made it clear that the main battle in prospect was the GLC election. Over the next few months *Briefing* played an important role in the left's campaign by providing ammunition against right-wingers (including names of Labour councillors who 'voted with the Tories' on council spending cuts) and details of progress on the manifesto and selection. Its early contributors included many people who were to go on to become GLC councillors in 1981, including Tony Banks, Gareth Daniel, Bryn Davies, Andy Harris, Tony Hart, Lewis Herbert, Paul Moore and George Nicholson. They also included two of the

1983 intake of new Labour MPs, Jeremy Corbyn and Chris Smith. *Briefing* prided itself on an open-door editorial policy. It had 'editorial collective' meetings in Livingstone's room at County Hall which anyone could attend; and it was tolerant enough to carry an article by the right-winger McIntosh attacking *Briefing*'s 'tradition of giving pride of place to battles within the Labour Party, instead of to fighting the Tories' (*LLB* 8 February 1981).

The people at the core of the group, however, were Livingstone, Ted Knight (leader of Lambeth council), Corbyn (a NUPE official and member of the Labour regional executive), Chris Knight and Graham Bash (both members of Chartist). In spite of the open door, only tiny numbers of activists were involved. In the August 1980 issue, Chris Knight reported the launch of a 'major' campaign against Michael Heseltine's proposed Local Government Bill at a *Briefing* conference which was 'the largest rank-and-file gathering of this type for a number of years'. He explained: 'Over 200 delegates, from 30 CLPs and a dozen trades councils (amongst others) attended.'

People who have subsequently come to regard Livingstone as a populist politician should remember that the roots of his climb to power lie in an ability to emerge at the head of a very small pack.

This article by Chris Knight concluded by making a clear distinction between the *Briefing* group and ideological purists on the left: 'To the extent that we lack the physical power to overthrow the Tories and their system, we are *forced* to make difficult choices. The task isn't to pass resolutions "demanding" the impossible. It is to fight for real power. This is what those of us around *Briefing* are beginning to do.'

With organisational support from Livingstone and liaison through *Briefing*, the left made big advances in constituency selections of candidates. Some attempts were made to deselect sitting Labour members of the GLC who wanted re-election, but this was only achieved in three cases where special personal or local factors were at play. (One of these was in Bermondsey where the former GLC leader, Sir Reg Goodwin, was deselected for reasons of age and local Bermondsey politics which had

LONDON LABOUR BRIEFING

10p

No 2   MAY 1980

G.L.C. MANIFESTO:

THIS TIME WE'LL DECIDE!

JEREMY CORBYN
Member of GLRC Executive

TRADITIONALLY THE PRODUCTION of election manifestoes has been a process steeped in mysticism and intrigue—the actual document emerging from a "smoke-filled room" a few weeks before an election and thrust on the unsuspecting public and received with horror by an equally unsuspecting party membership.

The subjugation of the production of a document as vital as an election manifesto to the need to grab the headlines at the appropriate time has been a serious failing of the Labour Party. Even more disastrous has been the process that allows vital planks of Conference policy to be removed at the crucial stage by the Party leadership.

Had Labour won in 1979, Callaghan would not have been in the least embarrassed by Labour's programme. By a system of "closed door" arm-twisting he had defeated many of the vital conference votes of the preceeding five years. Any battle for a socialist manifesto is inseparable from the battle for real accountability and democracy in the Labour Party.

As a start we must remove the content and production of a manfiesto from the mysticism of the past and state quite clearly that our actual programme we intend to **implement** is the manifesto! Only by this process will the Party be forced to campaign on all its policies at all times. That way the public political education work can be seen to have a real definable aim.

The NEC has decided to produce a "rolling manifesto". This we all welcome, but it must be backed up with continuous campaigning in support of these policies.

In many ways, the battles that have been fought and lost nationally have been mirrored in London. The 1977 GLC manifesto was produced by a tiny caucus emanating from County Hall and was clearly not representative of GLRC Conference decisions. Our manifesto for 1981 will be different—it will be a socialist policy and will be voted on in its entirity by a full conference of the London Labour Party.

Immediately after the 1979 Conference of the London Labour Party, the newly-elected Executive appointed six working parties to deal with major areas of policy: Industry and Employment, Housing, Transport, Planning, Finance and Management, and Education. Membership of these committees was drawn from EC members, nominees from affiliated bodies and a small number of co-opted Party members.

Their brief is to produce policy documents in line with conference policy, also ones that could be used immediately by a Labour GLC to enact policy. It is now vital that no excuse for lethargy, welching on the manifesto or obstruction by Council officials should be tolerated. The record of the 1973-77 Labour GLC was indeed one of direct violation of the manifesto in the case of transport and of allowing the bureaucracy at County Hall to spend three and a half years delaying a planning policy that could not then be started before losing office. **CONTINUED ON PAGE TWO**

Editorial

Since we last went to press, a number of good things have happened. The T&GWU's demand for a recalled National Conference has been conceded, though how much a real discussion on strategy will occur remains to be seen.

Equally, at London level the GLRC has opened a major new battle in the fight for control of the GLC with its plans for free public transport. These will come under a vicious attack from the Tories, right-wingers in our own party, and, of course, the media. Members **must** ensure that these proposals are fought through—full support from the London Labour movement is essential.

It has been very clear for some time now that a major conference for socialists in local government must be organised. **Briefing** will undertake to help organise this and plans are now afoot. The next issue will carry full details but any enquiries and offers of help should be sent to Mike Davis (tel: 254 8601), who is acting as co-ordinator for this venture. The conference is provisionally booked for Saturday 5th July.

nothing to do with Livingstone or *Briefing*.) The left's success was mainly in filling vacant winnable constituencies. In these seats the tally was about three to one in favour of the left.

Livingstone himself switched constituencies again from Hackney North to Paddington, a key marginal. His argument was that he only wanted to be on the GLC if Labour was in power – which it only could be if marginals like Paddington were won. On the basis of 1979 general election results, Paddington was Labour's forty-third most winnable seat out of ninety-two London constituencies and it was only fifteen minutes walk from his West Hampstead home. Livingstone won the nomination in a close-fought contest with Jean Merriton, who was herself considered to be both competent and on the left and who had stood for Paddington in the 1977 GLC election. He was also in the running for the nearby marginal of Hampstead which Labour eventually lost. If the Paddington selection had not come through first, Livingstone might have taken Hampstead and never have become a councillor in 1981.

During the year before the polls, one of the most familiar sights at County Hall was Livingstone in safari-jacket, scurrying about with his lists of candidates, working out the latest likely tally in the leadership contest which would follow the 1981 election. By polling day he knew that, whatever Labour's possible majority, he was at least two or three votes short of the clear left majority which could have guaranteed his leadership victory. He therefore needed to pull over the votes of half a dozen older councillors in the Labour centre, most of whom were not a little nervous of the young activists from *Briefing*.

The Labour rump which had been left at County Hall after the electoral debacle of 1977 had plodded through another three years under the leadership of Sir Reg Goodwin. Its chief whip, the elfin-featured former Church of England canon Harvey Hinds, had received periodic complaints from senior members of the group that it was time Goodwin was put out to grass. But, as Hinds explains, nothing was done because 'the natural heir and successor was anathema to the elder statesmen'.

The natural heir was Illtyd Harrington, an exuberant Welsh-man prone to somewhat florid oratory, who had been the darling of the London left in the 1960s. The left had ostracised him after 1975 when, as GLC finance chairman, he had pushed through the Goodwin cuts package.

But Goodwin and the right also disapproved of him because they believed him to be unreliable – a judgment which was probably due more to his extravagant personal mannerisms than to his political aptitude or leanings. There was therefore a power vacuum (if that is not too grand a term) at the top of the GLC Labour group. Goodwin did not groom a young right-winger to replace him, preferring to place his confidences with bright young GLC officers rather than with any politicians.

The manner of Goodwin's departure is regarded by Hinds as typical of his aloof style. 'When I got back from holiday in April 1980, there was a large manilla envelope on my desk. Attached to it was a note in Reg's handwriting saying: "Inside you will find a letter which you will doubtless wish to distribute to all members of the Labour group." Inside the manilla envelope were twenty-eight photocopies of a letter of resignation . . . It was the first that I as chief whip knew about it.'

In the leadership election contest which followed, there were three candidates: Harrington, Livingstone and Andrew McIntosh (who was the natural candidate of the Labour right). Livingstone recalls: 'I did a head count. I had four votes. About a dozen were prepared to vote for Illtyd Harrington, but a reluctant majority would have ended up supporting Andrew McIntosh. I spent about two weeks trying to persuade most of the people planning to vote for Illtyd that he could not get a majority, whereas I could.'

Surprisingly Livingstone nearly pulled it off. Because of some incompetent tactical voting by members whose main purpose was to dish either Harrington or McIntosh, Livingstone emerged top of the first ballot with ten votes. Harrington and McIntosh tied with nine each. In the run-off for second place, Livingstone voted for McIntosh, whom he thought he had a better chance of beating subsequently. (This gave McIntosh sixteen votes to Harrington's twelve.) In the final ballot, McIntosh beat Livingstone by fourteen votes to thirteen, with two abstentions. Given the left's view of the County Hall Labour group as a bunch of right-wing dinosaurs, this was a remarkably good showing by Livingstone. The measure of his true support was shown in a later ballot for deputy leader when he got only seven votes to Harrington's twenty-one. Yet, with a certain amount of tactical footwork, he came within one vote of winning the leadership.

There is a second astonishing feature of the 1980 leadership contest. Livingstone was responsible for ending Harrington's chances. Yet Harrington and his campaign manager, Hinds, both voted for Livingstone in the final ballot and went on to provide him with the centre support he needed in 1981. This cannot have been for love of *London Labour Briefing*, which, reporting the 1980 contest in June, said: 'Even McIntosh's victory was preferable to the other main challenger of the right, Illtyd Harrington, whose style of politics we will not comment on as the law of libel can be harsh on small socialist magazines.'

So why did Harrington and Hinds back Livingstone? 'Our assessment of Andrew McIntosh was that he was just a very slightly cleverer version of Reg Goodwin,' says Hinds. 'Reg was a hermit. He lived entirely within himself. And as a leader he was weak. He was the prey to the last person who got into his room before the decision had to be taken . . . He had great expertise in financial matters and my own view is that he was a man of integrity, but a recluse, a sphinx, who couldn't socialise, couldn't talk to people, had to be bludgeoned into actually receiving anyone into his room . . .

'I, as his chief whip, almost had to make an appointment with his secretary to see him . . . Upon entry, he would be at one end of the room, deep in papers, and eventually he would look up. Then he would be absolute courteousness itself – do sit down, can I get you a cup of tea – but there was always the impression of actually intruding on private grief to walk into the room and bring him in contact with the reality of the political situation . . .'

Goodwin had had a lifetime's experience in local government. As leader of Bermondsey council from 1947 to 1965, he had been responsible for municipalising almost all its housing. 'He was a good local government member of the old-style type, determined to do good for the people . . . He was brought up in the old LCC tradition of the leader giving maximum attention to chief officers and minimum attention to elected members' concerns. Members were in a sense a hindrance, a nuisance, like flies which have to be swatted every so often. And the group he had to lead were mostly brought up in the same tradition and accepted it . . .

'When Reg made a speech in the council chamber on whatever subject, particularly finance and the budget, it was always superb . . . carefully thought-out, carefully prepared, in private, in silence, with able briefing from [officers]. But in the rough and tumble of the Labour group, Reg as a leader was an absolute disaster.'

So why did Hinds feel that McIntosh, a bustling middle-aged market researcher, would follow Goodwin's example? 'One of Andrew's weaknesses was that he was too clever by half . . . If I had ever become leader of a Labour group, I would never go to the length of having one of those super rolls of lavatory paper – greaseproof paper on a board – so that I could scribble on it in large letters, turn it over and do the next page, and explain to people, in words of one syllable – because they are so idiotic, because they couldn't possibly understand it unless they had it before their very eyes – why the rate precept should be 20p in the pound or whatever. Andrew is essentially, I think, an academic and he made the great mistake of talking down to the Labour group and to the regional Labour Party on a number of occasions . . . You do not lecture the Labour Party. You do not talk down to the Labour Party.'

But was not Livingstone's style of activist politics equally distasteful? 'Ken was a leader who knew his mind and knew what he wanted to achieve . . . [After Reg] I was yearning for a leader who would lead . . . I saw in the likes of Ken and the young people who were just beginning to come through in my local Labour Party the best hope for the future of the Labour Party,' says Hinds.

Harrington has another explanation: 'What struck all the older politicians was the speed and efficiency of what we were looking at. We overestimated it [the advance of the left] very much. We thought we were looking at a juggernaut. We were looking at something that was sharper, younger, appeared to be crisper . . . They looked unstoppable. They appeared to be fresh, open-minded. These were attractive things to see. We had gone through a long period of appalling local government. It had atrophied . . . Things needed to be done in transport, housing, fresh ideas about planning. They all appeared to be alive, marvellously alive.'

And so by May 1981, the centre was ready to seek rejuvenation by going for an exhilarating rise on the bandwagon of the left. As Harrington puts it: 'It had flags, whistles, and steam coming out of it at you.'

Livingstone says that when he lost the leadership in 1980, he initially thought that McIntosh would be leader for a decade: 'He started to accommodate to the left. He went along with what was going in the manifesto. He recommended my appointment as planning and transport spokesman. But then, about June, I realised things weren't working for him. The centre who had voted for Illtyd had largely not been won over by him. He had made no effort to sit down with Illtyd or Harvey and involve them. He actually just worked with me. They felt isolated and out of it. And they never had liked him terribly much. So I started to work quite closely with them . . . by mid-July we knew that we had the votes to get rid of Andrew.'

Needless to say, McIntosh (who resents being called aloof, although he admits being 'shy') thinks Harrington and Hinds are rather too good at inventing rationalisations for what he believes was a sell-out to gain senior jobs in the administration. But this may underestimate how close the two men came to Livingstone in the year before the 1981 election. By then both had developed an almost fatherly affection for the prodigal left-winger, his domestic crises (this was the period of his separation from his wife Christine), and his endless supply of little lists of the latest state of play in the constituencies. If not part of his family, they gradually became part of his team.

So, as Labour went into the election, Livingstone had achieved two objectives. Constituency selections had secured nearly enough left-wingers to ensure an overall left majority on the GLC

Labour group. And his personal qualities had won over the additional votes necessary from the old-guard centre, provided nothing happened to jeopardise their support. There was a third crucial strand of preparation – the battle over the manifesto.

'I know you keep reading that manifestos aren't important – that they are only read by politicians. But they are the key to what happens after an election,' says Livingstone. 'Take the document produced by the Labour Party for the 1983 general election. It really is very good. It could justify everything a Benn government would want to do. It could also unfortunately justify everything a Healey government would want to do. It is sufficiently vaguely worded. Whereas our 1981 one was absolutely precise. Mind you, it was also fifty thousand words long.'

The process of drawing up the manifesto began in June 1979, nearly two years before the election. Whereas past manifestos had been criticised by the left because they were 'imposed' by the people at the top of the GLC and London Labour Party hierarchy, this exercise involved so much consultation that only the most energetic party members could stand the pace.

The regional executive set up a series of working parties to produce policies for each main area of GLC activity. Party members were able to read their draft reports and attend meetings to discuss them. The output was then submitted to a special conference of the London party in October 1980 for amendment and ratification. This exhaustive and exhausting procedure gave considerable power to the handful of people who were prepared to do the work. Livingstone acknowledges: 'The right wing were very unlucky at this time, in that Reg Goodwin never really put much effort into anything . . . He didn't oppose the more demo- cratic method of drawing up the manifesto. No one could. It's like opposing freedom, isn't it? And there was no group of talented young right-wingers rushing around doing any leg work for him.'

For Livingstone, the big breakthrough was winning a vote on the regional executive (on the casting vote of Arthur Latham) to become chairman of the transport working party. 'That was the key position to be in, because all the major rows were going to be on the amount we subsidised London Transport. That put me in a fairly strong position and the focus of a lot of attention within the party in that crucial period.'

Until then, Livingstone's links with the trade unions had been limited. He had not participated much in the industrial side of the movement except by way of one-off alliances during disputes in which he was involved as a councillor; and he had been hostile to the trade union hierarchy which tended to vote against everything he proposed on the London regional executive.

It was essential, however, that the unions supported the GLC manifesto both in general terms and – perhaps even more important – in terms of the specific items which affected their members' interests. Livingstone's links with the TUC and transport unions at this stage helped him to build up another important part of his political network.

There was great disagreement about what the GLC public transport policy should be. Most people on the left of the party wanted LT to move over to a policy of free fares to encourage maximum use of the bus and Underground system and to provide maximum benefit to passengers at the expense of ratepayers. The unions, however, were concerned that abolition of fares would mean abolition of ticket collectors' and bus conductors' jobs. They also feared that the LT infrastructure could not cope with a sudden massive increase in passenger demand. Meanwhile the Labour right were worried about the rate implications of un-limited subsidies to public transport. They agreed that fares were too high, but they wanted to fix an appropriate level of subsidy and then let fares rise with inflation.

Livingstone, who had previously argued for free fares, gradually moved over to a compromise plan whereby fares would be cut by 25 per cent and then frozen in cash terms so that the impact of the policy would grow as inflation took its toll on the value of money. He did not, however, feel confident that either the left, the unions, or the right would accept this conclusion. So his working party fudged the issue, by producing options for discussion by the party, representing the three main strands of opinion. Even by the time of the special regional conference in October 1980, it was by no means clear which side would win. Livingstone's speech in favour of the compromise solution was widely regarded as masterful and decisive in determining that the compromise won a clear majority.

The total manifesto which emerged was never fit for public consumption. It was ridiculously long and in parts repetitive, meaningless or badly written. But it fulfilled all of Livingstone's basic objectives. It provided specific pledges for action by the incoming Labour GLC which were so cast-iron that there could be no excuses for backsliding. Its clear promises were limited to policies which it was feasible to implement. Other items were included – such as the Militant resolution that 'a Labour GLC will demand that the next Labour Government will immediately . . . nationalise the banks and . . . annul local authorities' debts, with compensation being paid only on the basis of any proven need of the share and bond holders'. But in each case these 'impossible' items were expressed as the GLC calling for action rather than being committed to implement anything itself.

Livingstone regards the manifesto preparation as the key to maintaining unity in the Labour group after the election. 'Nobody dares to dissent from the manifesto because everyone was involved in drawing it up.'

Apart from the cheap fares commitment, the other main items in the manifesto were: to form a Greater London Enterprise Board to revive the London economy and create ten thousand new jobs a year by 1984/5; to restore the GLC's strategic housing role, halt the voluntary sale of council houses, and freeze council rents, at least for the first year of office; to stop the spread of office development in central London, using GLC planning powers to encourage alternative development of housing, open space and light industry; to discourage further road building; and to terminate 'wasteful expenditure on so-called home defence'.

By the time of the election in May 1981, all Livingstone's political networks were in place. Through *London Labour Briefing* he had formed links with many of the left activists in the constituencies. Through the process of drawing up the manifesto, he had established better contacts with the unions. Through his relations at County Hall, he had attracted vital support from the old-guard GLC Labour centre. In this whole elaborate network, Livingstone was the only common link. By election day he had pieced together the alliance which was to deliver him power. On May 8, 1981, the voters did the rest.

Livingstone concludes: 'In retrospect it really was a question of being the right person in the right place at the right time. If I hadn't been here, Andrew [McIntosh] most probably would have survived, because I doubt if anybody else would have pulled it all together. But it was so easy to pull together. The party was ready for it to happen.'

5 · Salamander Days

Fleet Street took several weeks to decide whether 'Red Ken' was a threat to civilisation as they knew it or a harmless and rather quirky figure of fun.

The mainstream press had been hostile to the caucus coup which brought him the leadership on May 9 and suspicious about changes to the council's standing orders which were introduced at the first available opportunity to help Labour get its business through unhindered by its relatively slim majority.

There was some alarm about the GLC's early threat (later withdrawn) to suspend £550,000 of grants to the Royal Opera House, Covent Garden, and redistribute the money to grassroots organisations like community arts centres. There was also suspicion prompted by the decision to reject an invitation for their leader to attend the Royal Wedding between Prince Charles and Lady Diana Spencer later that summer. Livingstone was quoted in the *Observer*: 'I would like to see the abolition of the monarchy, replacing it with an elected president who would be ceremonial ... Some of the characters who are hangers-on and living off public expense are really quite revolting ... What earthly use the country gets out of Princess Anne I really don't know.'

On May 28, *London Labour Briefing* published its victory issue under the headline LONDON'S OURS, in which Livingstone pledged to use County Hall as an open campaigning base to bring down the Thatcher government.

Two days later the GLC provided accommodation and food for five hundred young people who had arrived in London from the north on the People's March for Jobs. As the *Morning Star* pointed out on May 27: 'The marchers will sleep in County Hall on camp beds originally intended for use as part of the council's civil defence programme, which has been abandoned by the new administration.' There followed stories about how the GLC was to spend £400,000 on a council newspaper to be distributed free to all Londoners ('It's propaganda on the rates' – *Daily Mail*, June 6); and about how responsibility allowances were to be divided up among the administration's central team of 'full-time' councillors.

Most of this early coverage was critical and it was strongly personalised around Livingstone, in spite of his protestations about the more collective style of leadership which Labour had introduced. On May 30 the *Daily Mail* carried a feature by David Norris under the headline THE COMMISSAR OF COUNTY HALL. On the surface, Livingstone was as straight-talking as they come, proud of his working class origins and easy-going man of the people image, he wrote. 'Underneath the real Mr Livingstone is as elusive as the disappearing natterjack toad – a threatened species which the 35-year-old part-time conservationist is fighting to protect.' Livingstone might sound eminently reasonable in his arguments on subjects like the need to control the GLC bureaucracy. 'It is only when he goes on to offer his own socialist solution to the problem that the mask of reason and moderation begins to slip and the face of a dogmatic zealot peers through.'

Even the right-wing papers, however, found it hard to sustain this menacing tone when they were also deriving light entertainment from Livingstone's lifestyle. 'The harsh realities of life confront Kenneth Livingstone soon after he crawls from under his pink-patterned duvet in the simple bed-sitting room, which shakes every time a train passes on the Bakerloo line below,' began Brian Silk in the *Daily Telegraph* ('Bedsitter vision of the Socialists' Mr London', June 15). 'At 36 he is the leader of the Greater London Council, with responsibility for more people than any local authority in Europe and even some sovereign states. But at the £20 a week room in Maida Vale he is just one of the tenants who have to share the lavatory. To the neighbours he is the bizarre character who spends his free time searching the local terrain for slugs and woodlice to feed his seven pet lizards.' This account of Livingstone's day ended '. . . close to midnight when Livingstone comes up the steps at Maida Vale station and stops to buy a packet of chips on the way to his room and his seven cold-blooded friends.'

It was these pets – salamanders acquired when he and his wife Christine took a party of schoolchildren to France in 1976 – which were used to reduce Livingstone to the level of a music-hall joke. They popped up from time to time in most of the newspapers and became a popular catchphrase guaranteed to raise a laugh.

John Mortimer, in a *Sunday Times* interview (July 19), produced the most sophisticated mickey-taking of this period when he reported a conversation with Livingstone and The Chair (Valerie Wise, vice chair of the industry committee). 'The atmosphere in the tea room had been one of suppressed excitement, with smiles and jokes, as when a crowd of dedicated young people get together to produce, with tireless enthusiasm, a television show, or a repertory production, or, indeed, a system of local government,' he wrote. The future might remember Livingstone as 'another finally moderate GLC leader whose bush jackets and salamanders have sunk into the oak-panelled history of County Hall like the ancient whiff of Herbert Morrison's pipe tobacco.'

So was Livingstone a dangerous Trot or a figure of fun? Most newspapers made up their minds on or about Tuesday July 21, when Livingstone entertained the mother of one of the IRA hunger-strikers from the H-blocks of the Maze prison near Belfast. During the early days of his leadership, Livingstone had already been making a series of statements in favour of the withdrawal of British troops from Northern Ireland and in support of the hunger-strikers who were demanding conditions akin to political status. Nonetheless the visit of Mrs Alice McElwee, whose son Thomas was on the forty-fourth day of his fast, created an explosive impact.

Livingstone told the *Standard* (July 21) that he wanted to break Britain's bi-partisan policy on Northern Ireland and to commit the Labour Party to a policy of withdrawal. 'The H-block protest is part of the struggle to bring about a free, united Ireland,' he said. 'They have my support, and they have the support of the majority of the Labour Party rank and file. I have been consistently in favour of withdrawal from Ireland and to get away from the idea that it is some sort of campaign against terrorism. It is in fact the last colonial war.'

The incident was condemned by the Conservative leader, Sir Horace Cutler, as self-seeking publicity by Livingstone which had nothing to do with the GLC. Livingstone replied: 'We have a large Irish community who live in fear of intimidation by the police and the security forces. You can go to any pub in Kilburn and actually see the Special Branch sitting there with their ears flapping, looking for any scrap of evidence they can use' (*Daily Express*, July 22). He told a press conference that the bipartisan Tory-Labour approach to Northern Ireland had led to over two thousand deaths 'and a campaign of repression the like of which has not existed anywhere else in the world . . . The eventual freedom and unity of Ireland for the whole working class is a major blow against international capitalism and the rulers of our state' (*News Line*, July 22).

Livingstone explained that Mrs McElwee had been invited by a fellow GLC councillor, Andy Harris, a member of the Labour Committee on Ireland, to give members of the Labour group accurate information about the position of the H-block hunger-strikers following the death of Bobby Sands (*Daily Mail*, July 22).

It was this episode which marked the end of Livingstone's salamander days in the media. Thomas McElwee had received sentences of 141 years after being convicted in 1976 of being a member of an eight-man IRA team which exploded seventeen bombs in Ballymena. In conventional political terms, Livingstone's support for his cause (without at that stage condemnation of his act of terrorism) was widely considered to be outrageous.

'In his brief spell on the stage, the insufferable Mr Livingstone has proved himself a menace to stability in public life,' said the first of a series of increasingly vitriolic leaders in the *Sun* on July 23.

On the evening of the McElwee visit, Livingstone told a meeting of the full GLC council that he knew the names of two policemen who were connected with the murder of Blair Peach, a young New Zealand schoolteacher who had died in the Southall riots two years before. 'It will not increase respect for law and order if members of the Special Patrol Group are allowed to get away with murder,' Livingstone said. 'It is known, I think, to

almost every left-wing organisation in this country the names of
two individuals, one of whom was responsible for the murder of
Blair Peach. It would be irresponsible to announce both names
because clearly one did not murder Blair Peach and the other did'
(*Standard*, July 22).

The next day Livingstone warned a private meeting of London's Labour borough leaders that if the GLC fulfilled its full
manifesto programme, its rates could rise by 120 per cent in the
spring. His remark was leaked to the press by one of the borough
leaders, most of whom were right-wing opponents of Livingstone
within the Labour Party, and all of whom faced borough elections
the following May. 'The GLC is in a Walt Disney situation,' John
O'Grady, then Labour leader of Southwark, told the *Standard* on
July 23.

It was this build-up of stories which finally drew the concentrated firepower of Fleet Street. The *Daily Mail* comment column
of July 24 catalogued the events of Livingstone's week and
concluded: 'Mr Livingstone is a doctrinaire clown. But there is
little laughing now at the Rake's Progress on which he is leading
the Kingdom's capital city. It is a grotesque portent of things to
come; of what could happen to all of us if we let the New Left
misrule Britain tomorrow as they are misruling London today.'

The papers that day also reported Mrs Thatcher's denunci-
ation in the Commons of Livingstone's support for the IRA
hunger strikers: 'If those reports are true, it is the most disgraceful
statement I have ever heard,' she said (*Guardian*, July 24).

And in its editorial column the *Standard* observed: 'People, they
say, get the politicians they deserve. Yet surely no one – but no one
– deserves Mr Ken Livingstone. His rule at the Greater London
Council goes straight into the cruel-and-unnatural-punishment
class.'

From then on there was an almost daily diet of Livingstonia in
the press. The day before the Royal Wedding he welcomed eight
demonstrators from the H-Blocks Armagh Committee who kept
up a forty-eight hour fast and vigil on the steps of County Hall
during the national celebrations. 'I can't think of a more appalling
contrast between this wedding beanfeast and what is happening in

Ireland,' Livingstone said, as the demonstrators prepared to release hundreds of black balloons over London during the wedding procession (*Daily Mail*, July 29). Below this story it was reported that the London borough of Bromley was planning court action against the GLC supplementary rate, due on October 1, to pay for its fares cut.

It was at this stage that rumblings of disaffection started to surface within the Labour group, alarmed that their manifesto programme was being jeopardised by Livingstone's projection in the media. Minutes of a GLC Labour group meeting on July 27 record under any other business: 'Public relations: There was a general discussion on the issues of press coverage with particular reference to the 120 per cent rate increase story and the support given by the Leader and other members to the H-Block Committee.

'Reference was made to the expression of views by the Leader, distracting attention from the work of the Council. The Leader pointed out that he did not arrange for Mrs McElwee to visit County Hall and that the rate story had become public despite the fact that he had only spoken about it at a private meeting. Other Members referred to the need to avoid the excesses of the Cutler years . . . The point was made that the Group had a responsibility to the party to show that the programme on which all are agreed can be put into practice and be made to work.'

This pressure on Livingstone was, however, defused by the break-up of the council for the summer holidays. There was also some confidence that the group's newly-recruited political press officer, Veronica Crichton, might in future be able to project more positive aspects of the Labour administration's performance.

Livingstone went off for a fortnight with his wife Christine to Hongkong, Bangkok and Canton. (By then they had separated, but were still on friendly terms.) When he returned, it immediately became obvious that he was unable or unwilling to tone down his public utterances.

The Livingstone media circus resumed on August 18 with his speech to the Harrow Gay Unity Group where he announced: 'Everyone is bisexual. Almost everyone has the sexual potential for

"Eighty-six years ago Oscar Wilde got sent to prison for it, fourteen
years ago it was made legal, under Ken Livingstone it's going to be
compulsory!" *Standard*, August 20, 1981 (*Jak*)

anything.' He accused the police of planting decoys at well-known
gay hangouts (*Sun*, August 19).

'At this point the clown ceases to amuse and Londoners can
only hope that, having elected this weird creature, the law and Mr
Heseltine will somehow contrive to keep his wilder inclinations
within something like reasonable bounds,' said the *Daily Mail* on
August 20. In the same issue it sought out the views of three
psychologists on Livingstone's need to shock to gain attention. 'As
an only son and with both parents forced to hold down two jobs in
order to survive, it is most likely that he suffered a lack of attention.
Probably the only way he could get it was to be a naughty boy –
which he still acts like,' said one. The psychologists complained
they had been misquoted, but the Press Council later upheld the
conduct of the *Mail*.

It is hard to do justice to the sheer volume of anti-Livingstone press coverage by merely recounting some of its riper examples. He received a series of warnings from his colleagues, culminating in a dressing down from the group's whips, including left-wing allies such as Valerie Wise and John McDonnell. But Livingstone could not keep his mouth shut.

In a phone-in on London Broadcasting on August 23, he acknowledged that the Labour group was talking about 'ways of avoiding this press obsession with me'. But as Godfrey Barker of the *Daily Telegraph* reported the next day: 'There are no signs that he will take the obvious way of keeping quiet. In an hour of vintage Livingstone . . . he predicted a coup in Britain, declared that Northern Ireland "does not exist", said that Mr Owen Carron, the new anti-H-block MP, was welcome at County Hall and that calling the IRA "criminals and murderers" was nonsense. Then he called for legal controls on the Press, described New York as "an abominable place to live", announced that tourists were taking over parts of London, said that Labour councils "went through agonies" trying to reduce the rates and that he personally totally opposed rate increases. Later he relaxed over a glass of sherry and told me he was baffled by Press interest in him . . .'

Barker reported the next day: 'Labour calm has not been aided by the discovery that Mr Livingstone's speaking list for the rest of the year looks, as he put it, "as if I'm running for president". He is booked to speak at nearly every student union. Speaking and spending three hours nightly answering his postbag eats up a good deal of his 70-hour week . . .'

On August 30, David Lipsey reported in the *Sunday Times* that Labour leaders on London borough councils planned to send a round-robin letter demanding the resignation of 'rent-a-quote' Livingstone for fear of damage to Labour's chances in the borough elections the following May. The article pointed out that several GLC Labour right-wingers were potential defectors to the SDP and that four such defections would be enough to overturn Labour's overall majority.

On the same day, Tony Craig reported in the *Observer* on a radio interview he had conducted for the British Forces' Broadcasting Service in which Livingstone told him: 'If I was to make an

appeal, what I would say to everybody who's got arms in Northern
Ireland, whether they are in the British Army or the IRA, is to put
those arms down and go back to your home.'

There followed calls for Livingstone to be prosecuted for
sedition (*Daily Mail*, September 2) and a remark by the former
leader, Andrew McIntosh, that Livingstone's distracting behaviour was enabling Conservatives to convince the public that the
authority was run by 'a bunch of loonies who need to be kept under
control at all costs' (*Guardian*, August 31). In an editorial the
Guardian commented: 'If present trends continue, a point may be
reached some time next year where it will no longer be possible to
switch on Radio Tashkent without finding Mr Livingstone dron-
ing amiably away about (say) the British Israelite Movement or the
future of handloom weaving in an increasingly faceless technological society. Now some County Hall colleagues are desperately
casting about for some way to stop the ceaseless flow. Too late: the
County Hall caterpillar is too far embarked on the transformation
to media butterfly . . .' The *Guardian* observed: 'Mr Livingstone
could now be left to establish his personal court on the South
Bank, adding what he can to the public stock of entertainment,
controversy and understanding of the reptile world, while others
get on with the boring old job of governing London.'

Amid all this media frenzy, one trivial episode sticks most firmly
in the minds of Livingstone's aides. During a BBC Radio London
phone-in on September 10, Livingstone was again defending the
Labour group's decision that he should not attend the Royal
Wedding.

Staff at Radio London were convinced that he said: 'People
elect local councillors to do something about the housing problems and the transport problems, not to go swanning around at
these sort of . . . um . . . ceremonial occasions.' A Press Association reporter was sure he had said 'bum ceremonial occasions'.
GLC staff spent much of the day vainly trying to persuade
newspapers that it was an um, not a bum, and so did not merit
coverage. Livingstone's reputation was such, however, that no one
really believed them.

By this stage Livingstone's projection in the press was widely believed to be contributing to Labour's slump in popular support. It was the period of the meteoric growth of the SDP. Its leader, Roy Jenkins, had narrowly missed victory in the Warrington by-election in July; and the budding SDP-Liberal Alliance came briefly to have the appearance of an unstoppable electoral force. It was also the period of the campaign for Tony Benn to become deputy leader of the Labour Party under its new electoral college rules. Benn was out of action ill during that summer and Livingstone believes he attracted more critical coverage because he became a surrogate figure for attacks on Benn and the left.

Press interest in Livingstone did not, however, let up after Benn's narrow defeat at the Brighton party conference in September. Indeed his worst media showing was still to come.

On Saturday October 10, an IRA gang exploded a nail bomb outside the Irish guards barracks in Chelsea. Mrs Norah Field, a 61-year-old Pimlico widow, was killed after a six-inch nail had penetrated her heart. Thirty-nine other people, including children, were injured. It was the worst IRA terrorist outrage on the British mainland since the mid 1970s. The following Monday Livingstone was giving a talk to the Cambridge University Tory Reform Group. According to the report in the *Times* (October 13) he said of the terrorists responsible for the attack: 'They are not criminals or lunatics running about. That is to misunderstand them.' The *Times* explained that Livingstone told a student who pressed him for his views on IRA terrorism: 'Nobody supports what happened last Saturday in London. But what about stopping it happening? As long as we are in Ireland, people will be letting off bombs in London. I can see that we are a colonial power holding down a colony. For the rest of time violence will recur again and again as long as we are in Ireland. People in Northern Ireland see themselves as subject peoples. If they were just criminals or psychopaths they could be crushed. But they have a motive force which they think is good . . .'

The *Sun* used half its front page for a comment headlined THIS DAMN FOOL SAYS BOMBERS AREN'T CRIMINALS, which blasted out: 'This morning the *Sun* presents the most odious man

THE Sun

day, October 13, 1981   12p   TODAY'S TV: PAGE 12

This damn fool says the bombers aren't criminals

Red Ken Livingstone . . . *leader of the Greater London Council*

PAGE ONE OPINION

Sun, October 14, 1981

in Britain. Take a bow, Mr Ken Livingstone, Socialist leader of the Greater London Council.

'In just a few months since he appeared on the national scene, he has quickly become a joke. Now no one can laugh at him any longer. The joke has turned sour, sick and obscene. For Mr Livingstone steps forward as the defender and apologist of the criminal, murderous activities of the IRA.' The *Sun* continued with the same quotes provided in the *Times* and commented: 'Among the Socialist members of the GLC there must be many who are as outraged and disgusted by Mr Ken Livingstone as the rest of us. While he continues as their leader he is making the very name "Socialist" stink in people's nostrils. They should kick him out. And right this minute.'

The *Daily Mail* followed suit, concluding its editorial with the observation: 'This is the behaviour of a man who through Marxist dogma has become an alien in his own country, blind to the IRA's bloodiest crimes when even committed on his own doorstep. He is certainly not fit to rule Britain's capital city.'

And the *Daily Express*: 'Ever since he sneaked into power under cover of a moderate Labour leadership, Mr Livingstone has spoken and acted in what – with an excess of charity – may be called an eccentric fashion. He has upset everyone from boycotting royalty, to ravaging the ratepayers. But enough is enough. The conscience of the whole country is affronted by his remarks about the IRA bombing. If the London Labour group does not repudiate him immediately, the public will draw only one conclusion – that his fellow Labour councillors agree with him. Then Labour, not only in the capital, but throughout the land, will be branded as wholly unworthy.'

These editorials and associated news stories appeared on the morning of a regular GLC council day. It is difficult to think of any other such vitriolic expressions of opinion against a contemporary politician. Livingstone called a press conference to condemn this coverage as 'ill-founded, utterly out of context and distorted'. He announced that he would be taking action against the *Sun* over its 'most odious man in Britain' editorial. (This gave the *Sun* the opportunity for another unapologetic page-one editorial headlined NOW THE DAMN FOOL IS TAKING US TO THE PRESS COUNCIL.)

At the council meeting Livingstone explained that he condemned all violence and he stood for one minute's silence with the rest of the council as a mark of sympathy for the victims of the bombing. But he re-asserted his view that if the IRA were treated simply as criminals, the problem would not be solved.

Sir Horace Cutler, GLC Conservative leader, successfully requisitioned a special council meeting for the following week to censure Livingstone for 'misusing his position to further his extreme views on subjects over many of which the council has no jurisdiction'. And a round-robin letter from twenty members of the Labour group was delivered to the chief whip, Harvey Hinds, expressing strong dissatisfaction with Livingstone's recent refer-

"There you are, Ken, not everybody's against you!" *Daily Express*,
October 24, 1981 (*Jak*)

ences to the Irish situation after his pledge during the summer that
he would concentrate on London affairs and not allow media
interest in his other opinions to distract public attention from what
the GLC was trying to do.

During the day it also became known that, the night before, the
Labour group had by only a narrow majority refused to accept as
emergency business a letter from John McDonnell suggesting it
should meet with representatives of the IRA and INLA to try to
negotiate peace in London (*Guardian*, October 14). Labour
members had not at that point known of Livingstone's remarks in
Cambridge or how they would be reported. When news of the
meeting emerged, however, it was taken as further evidence of
Labour members' eccentric behaviour over the Irish issue. That
day too a second victim of the Chelsea nail-bombing, eighteen-
year-old John Patrick Breslin, died from his injuries. He was an
Irish Catholic civilian.

Over the week that followed, there was mounting pressure on
Livingstone. On Thursday October 15 he was attacked in the
street and sprayed with red paint from an aerosol can while he was
on his way to talk to a meeting of businessmen in the City.

On the Friday he cancelled a speaking engagement at a pro-
IRA rally the following day. IRA supporters staged a demon-

Labour Herald, January 29, 1982

stration outside an office in Kilburn where he was holding a political surgery to try to get him to change his mind (*Daily Mail*, October 17).

But Livingstone survived. He got united support from his Labour group the following Wednesday for an amendment, drafted by Frances Morrell, which defused Cutler's censure motion. It asked the council to place on record its deep sense of outrage at terrorist acts of violence in London, which had resulted in bloodshed and the loss of innocent lives. It also regretted that the Opposition and Conservative newspapers had given exaggerated attention to the views of individual Labour members in order to distract attention from the threat to jobs, living standards and services of the people of London posed by Mrs Thatcher's disastrous economic policy. It added that the council committed itself to continue to carry out the programme on which Labour was elected and to defend the people of London from punitive measures by the Environment Secretary, Michael Heseltine, by a campaign of total opposition to his legislation. This was carried by 45 votes to 39 (*Guardian*, October 22).

The *Sun* led its front page on the same day with the story headlined RED KEN'S REPRIEVE. The *Times* reported that the price of this reprieve was spelt out in a strong speech by Illtyd Harrington, the deputy leader, who said: 'Today the GLC is extricating itself from Northern Ireland. It is beyond any doubt that the leadership of this council is now going to concentrate on the constitutional problems coming from central government. This meeting today marks a watershed. We have taken a decision that we are going to get back on to a sane and sensible line.' In fact the reprieve had no price tag attached and Harrington's prognosis did not prove correct. Livingstone was embroiled in links with Sinn Fein at frequent intervals over the next two years. On each occasion he provoked massive press attention and hostility. As far as this book is concerned, however, it is time to break off from a description of the media's treatment of Livingstone to examine its consequences.

The first and most obvious came the day after the GLC censure debate when Bill Pitt won the Croydon North West by-election for the Liberal-SDP Alliance, taking 40 per cent of the vote, compared with a Liberal share of only 10.5 per cent in the 1979 general election. Labour was beaten into third place. Pitt commented: 'Mr Livingstone was directly responsible for this; and he signifies the drift of the Labour Party towards the kind of policies which people simply cannot accept. He was the unacceptable face of Socialism. During the campaign, the people on the doorsteps were disgusted and outraged about his comments on the IRA. It's appalling that he should have said what he did' (*Standard*, October 23). Labour leaders were also blaming the GLC's supplementary rate increase, which landed on voters' doormats during the campaign, and the divisive effects of Tony Benn's deputy leadership bid. In reality, it is hard to separate these specific problems for Labour from the general upward surge of the Alliance at that stage. But the episode cemented hostility to Livingstone within wide sections of the Parliamentary Labour Party.

On October 29, Anne Sofer won a GLC by-election for the SDP in St Pancras North, a previously impregnable Labour stronghold. She had been elected as a Labour member, but had resigned her seat to join the SDP. Sofer took 43.6 per cent of the vote, compared with 9.9 per cent gained by the Liberal the previous May.

Livingstone now acknowledges that during the autumn of 1981 he frequently doubted his capacity to continue as leader. 'I realised that there was a likelihood of a strong challenge at the group elections the following May. It was only the lack of an effective challenger that made me assume that at the end of the day I would most probably survive. You could get a majority of people to agree that the publicity was bad and that I might be mishandling it. You had great problems when you had to put together a majority of people in agreement that someone was going to be better than me.'

There were repeated rumours about six imminent defections to the SDP threatening Labour's overall majority. (In the end only Paul Rossi, member for Lewisham East, joined Anne Sofer.) There were doubts about the GLC's financial position – whether the Labour right could be persuaded to accept rate increases large enough to satisfy the left that manifesto commitments were not being sacrificed to expediency. And members of Livingstone's own senior team were making no effort to disguise their view that his rent-a-quote style was to blame for their devastatingly bad showing in the press and the opinion polls. It should not be forgotten that the Cambridge speech in which he said that the IRA were 'not just criminals' came only a week after the GLC had cut London Transport fares by 32 per cent – the showpiece of Labour's manifesto on which every effort should have been made to concentrate attention.

As it turned out, Livingstone's crucifixion in the media formed the basis of his subsequent political strength and popularity. He became such a controversial figure that he began to get half-hour interview slots on television programmes whose producers realised that he helped their ratings. These appearances allowed viewers to form their own opinions about him and to contrast them with the reputation that had been handed down to them that he was the 'most odious man in Britain'.

Livingstone has one of the best television styles of any contemporary politician. This can only partly be explained by his own analysis: 'I belong to the first generation of political leaders who were brought up watching the box. This gives us a tremendous advantage over people like Roy Jenkins whose lifestyle is such that he probably never watches if he can help it.'

In fact Livingstone's directness, self-deprecation, colourful language, complete unflappability under fire and lack of pomposity appealed to millions of people who were not at that stage supporters of his policies. This projection into television also coincided with a big change in news coverage. By Christmas 1981, the judgments from Lord Denning and the Law Lords against the GLC's cheap fares policy shifted the focus of debate on to the ground where the Labour administration most wanted it to be. Livingstone became a media star, projecting a popular image, defending fairly popular policies.

There are those who argue therefore that Livingstone was a brilliant self-publicist who courted the initial vilification to get himself into the public eye and who planned his projection with meticulous attention to detail. Sir Horace Cutler for instance says: 'He told me he learnt about public projection from me. You have to think. You have to produce ideas, some original, some way out, some gimmicky. Whatever it is, you make the news and the media will make you. You can be the most brilliant politician and never get noticed if you have no story that is newsworthy.' But this smacks of hindsight (with a dose of envy thrown in: Cutler craved the publicity which Livingstone eventually achieved).

Livingstone claims that his early projection in the press was unintended – the result of inexperience. 'I wasn't sufficiently capable as a politician of handling the media at that stage,' he says. 'I didn't realise what I have now come to realise that you have got to try and choose the ground on which what you say is presented to the media. You can't allow the media to set the framework of when issues are launched and raised.'

He argues that a lot of the press attention was either unpro-

'He told me he learnt about public projection from me . . .' – Sir Horace Cutler (*Guardian*)

voked or inaccurate. For example the Royal Wedding story leaked out in spite of a decision by the Labour group to avoid any fuss by simply asking the Palace not to send an invitation. The 120 per cent rate increase story was leaked by hostile Labour borough leaders when he was trying to give them private advice about their budget planning.

He is still angry about the infamous Cambridge speech and claims that the remark 'they are not criminals or lunatics running

. . . spot the clown (*Guardian*)

about' was 'too grammatically wrong' for him to have said. He maintains he was bending over backwards at the time to avoid controversy. Before he went to Cambridge, he had attended the opening press conference at the St Pancras North by-election and carefully ducked a question on the current situation in the Middle East on the grounds that it was not relevant to the GLC. 'I wasn't going to be caught like that. Then I tripped off to Cambridge and answered an honest question honestly. No one at the time thought it was unusual. It didn't go down badly at the Tory Reform Group. There were no gasps of horror in the audience.'

He says he did not know until later that there were two journalists present at the Cambridge meeting. One of them, Richard Holliday, was the *Daily Mail*'s full-time 'Red Ken watcher' and Livingstone says that his story, carried next day by the *Mail* in a relatively subdued fashion, was more accurate than the Press Association copy carried by the rest of Fleet Street. 'That was the last speech I made without a tape recorder for about eighteen months.'

Livingstone also bitterly resents the press intrusion into the lives of friends and relatives. At the start it was 'hilariously funny' to find a press photographer hiding behind his dustbin in the hope that he would come out in the morning with a companion who might be presumed to have stayed the night with him. But the harassment involved others. One reporter visited his mother in Lincoln professing to ask her views on the new Humber Bridge as an opening gambit to start her talking about her son. Another trapped the father of his ex-wife Christine into making derogatory comments about Livingstone during the divorce proceedings. Christine herself was offered and refused a large sum of money for selling her story. One of Livingstone's female aides at County Hall was disturbed early one Sunday morning by a reporter and photographer who had to be taken up to her bedroom before they were persuaded that Livingstone was not sleeping with her.

Later during the administration, Livingstone and Kate Allen, chair of Camden council women's committee, started a relationship which was also subjected to intrusive media scrutiny.

But whatever criticism Livingstone may have about individual stories and the behaviour of the press, he cannot deny that he failed to take action to stem the flow. His prime objective at the time was to show that the left could handle power and to ensure that the various factions in the Labour group stayed welded together. So why, after the initial press hysteria became obvious, did he continue to fuel it with off-the-cuff remarks which had no bearing on GLC administration?

'Don't forget there was another major motivation. Yes, the left have to show that they can run the GLC. We have to survive this administration. But we also have to show that we are different from what's happened in the past, that we aren't suddenly going to behave differently in office to the way we did before. Therefore if somebody who's asked me to speak on Ireland half a dozen times in the last ten years comes to me after the election and says, will you say so and so, I'm not going to behave differently. Because once you start down that route, immediately the whole of the activist wing of the party and beyond them the aware sections of the public are going to say: it's just the same old routine of getting into office, then changing and becoming establishment-minded. We don't have to worry about that now, because I think we have achieved in the public consciousness a perception that we are different from our predecessors. It was very important then. Everyone assumes that you have just got to hold the right with you. You haven't. You have got to hold the right and the left. And the left were the ones who had to absorb all the major setbacks and defeats in the first six to nine months.'

That might explain the quality of Livingstone's utterances, but surely not the quantity. Why allow the media-provocative opportunities to keep coming? 'It's not a question of allowing them. They do keep coming. It's a question of how you respond to them,' says Livingstone.

This answer does not seem to tell the whole of the story. His early exposure in the press was not so much due to the fact that he held firm to his earlier views when situations came up as to his availability and quotability. His diary for the period is full of interview appointments with journalists, many of them coming back for second helpings, having already rubbished him fulsomely in print.

Reporters who spent their lives squeezing half-quotable sentences out of very cautious and rather pompous public figures found Livingstone's laid-back style and colourful language an absolute gift. He seemed not to have been fitted with the restraining bolt which most politicians have installed somewhere between their minds and their mouths. It was not a question of listening through half an hour of boring clichés for the odd quotable phrase. Livingstone was quotable all through. He also talked in grammatical sentences. All you need to do to turn Livingstone speech into coherent written prose is to remove the 'ands' and 'buts' from the start of nearly every sentence and cut down on his excessive use of 'actually' and 'amazing'.

Reporters also enjoyed Livingstone's sense of fun. He emerged, for instance, from his first confrontation with the Transport Secretary, Norman Fowler, and told the waiting press: 'He asked to see me again. I think he must want me for my body.' Weightier politicians with weightier bodies do not say this sort of thing. Surely he realised that he was helping the media by providing them with ammunition for their attacks?

Livingstone's answer is: 'I'd spent all the time up until May 1981 trying to get any publicity at all for what I was doing and would get no more than a couple of mentions in the *Standard* in a good year. So all of my instincts were geared to getting any media attention whatsoever. During that period I had to try and re-educate myself to pushing off the media at a lot of points.

'Until you go through that near hysteria, I don't think that anything can prepare you for it or that you can be told the best way to handle it. You just have to learn from your mistakes as you go . . . It must be pretty much like one of those pop groups that suddenly has a hit. Bang, they go from total obscurity to being number one; and half of them end up dead within five years of overdoses and general indulgence . . .'

Livingstone also confesses that he found the early press coverage a bit of a joke and he sometimes took the mickey out of journalists, such as when he got the *Times* to report his views on why it was a socialist priority to eat All-Bran. 'It really was hilarious. People would fall around laughing until they realised that there were people out there actually believing it; and then they started to worry. No one could credit that degree of media interest. Everyone was going round vaguely bemused by it all . . . We just went through each week thinking: they will lose interest soon, they will go away, they can't possibly sustain all of this for much longer.'

Instead demands for interviews increased, reaching a peak around the time of the Royal Wedding. 'There were all these film crews from CBS, NBC, every television company in the world. They all seemed to want to do an interview about why I wasn't going to the Royal Wedding. It got to the point where it was taking too much time. So I said to Karen [Karen Brownridge, his personal assistant], I'm not doing any more interviews . . . About a day later she came in almost doubled up in hysterics. She said a woman television researcher had offered to go to bed with me if I'd do an interview about the Royal Wedding. We just fell about. I never did find out whether the offer was just to get through the secretarial barrier or whether it was really true.'

What would Herbert Morrison have said?

It is hard to escape the conclusion that Livingstone enjoyed riding the storm of media notoriety and that he revelled in his ability to withstand the buffeting. He remembers with pride the day (August 21, 1981) when Democratic Unionists (Protestants from Northern Ireland) brought over the Dunlop boys, orphans of an IRA atrocity, to embarrass him at County Hall. 'Nothing can be worse than the screaming media mob that day. I met journalists later who had been in the scrum pulling me backwards and forwards. They said they couldn't believe it, that it was terrifying. That doesn't terrify me or frighten me. If you can go through that, there is nothing they can actually do to you, I think. You just lead a much cleaner life than you might otherwise do.'

This capacity to soak up media punishment is an important attribute which most public figures discover they lack only when they reach a political or personal crisis in late career. Few can cope for more than a day or two with the media putting both their public and private lives under a spotlight.

But the result of Livingstone's love-hate relationship with the press was devastating for the morale of his Labour group. Their continued backing for him in crunch votes owed more to their distaste for the press vendetta than to any feelings of personal loyalty and warmth. Livingstone's exposure entirely obscured the policies which they were trying to implement and it offended against the principles of collective leadership which they wanted to adopt. As the Livingstone administration completed its first six months in office, it was foundering in a sea of press cuttings. If everything had been going well on the policy front, this might have been tolerable. But, as the next chapter will show, the GLC's chances of implementing its manifesto were by then looking distinctly dicey. In short, Livingstone's GLC was heading for a winter of internal discontent.

6 · Fog on the Heseltine

The media barrage was only one of the problems faced by the incoming Livingstone administration. Another came in the more glamorous shape of Michael Heseltine, then Secretary of State for the Environment. Heseltine was responsible for delivering the most difficult part of the spending cuts to which the Thatcher Government was committed. The 1979 Conservative manifesto had said: 'Any future government which sets out honestly to reduce inflation and taxation will have to make substantial economies, and there should be no doubt about our intention to do so.' Yet the party had made it clear that major areas of spending, such as defence, social security and the National Health Service, were to be protected from cuts. It was inevitable therefore that the burden would fall disproportionately on programmes such as housing, education and social services which were mainly provided by local government.

This was a problem. Under Denis Healey's Labour Chancellorship, techniques of controlling central government spending by setting cash limits on Whitehall departments and nationalised industries had been developed to a relatively fine art. But local councils' current expenditure was not subject to Treasury control. They had a long tradition of independence, with powers to fix their budgets and their rates which stretched back to Elizabethan times.

The Conservative party, at that stage, still set great store by tradition and professed opposition to the idea of a centralised state. Its leaders were not therefore immediately disposed to seek powers to take direct control of councils' spending. Heseltine, who was responsible for supervising local government in England, was also advised by officials that it would have been an administrative nightmare to intervene in the affairs of 413 separate local authorities.

Yet if the Government did not want to *control* the spending decisions of councils, it could nonetheless exert a powerful *influence* on their outcome. During the financial year 1979/80, when Heseltine took over, the English authorities were planning to spend £14 billion (nearly a quarter of all UK public spending). The Government funded 61 per cent of this in grants, leaving only 39 per cent to be found from domestic and business rate-payers.

There were no constitutional problems involved in any Government decision to reduce the proportion of this grant, which could be cash-limited like any other item of central expenditure. Many local authority treasurers expected it to be cut drastically in 1980/1. If that had been done, the councils would still have been free to maintain their spending if they chose; but a greater share of the cost would have been thrown on to the ratepayers. Since big rate increases are unpopular, most councils would probably have felt obliged to make the required spending cuts.

Heseltine, however, faced two problems with this strategy. The first was that he might be blamed just as much as the councils for forcing up the rates. This would have been particularly embarrassing because Mrs Thatcher had been personally involved in framing Tory manifesto pledges (explicit in 1974 and vague in 1979) to abolish domestic rates altogether. The second was that other Ministers (notably Mark Carlisle at Education) were concerned that some Tory councils were already spending so little that they were in danger of falling below basic minimum standards of service. Any generalised cut in grant could have produced damaging consequences in these areas.

Heseltine decided therefore that he wanted a system which withdrew grant from high-spending local authorities (which happened to be mainly in Labour control), but not from low spenders. This brought a heaven-sent opportunity for officials at the Department of the Environment (DoE) who had been trying unsuccessfully to persuade Ministers to reform the grant system since 1975. Within seven months of taking office in May 1979, Heseltine brought before Parliament a Local Government Planning and Land Bill which incorporated the civil servants' ideas for a new 'block grant'. After many legislative hiccups it became an Act in November 1980.

The block grant system provided the ground for a battle between central and local government which raged throughout the first Thatcher administration and into the second. Its introduction marked the start of a radical switch by central government from concern with total levels of local spending towards detailed intervention in the affairs of individual councils. The result for Livingstone's GLC was that it was forced to choose either to abandon its manifesto promises or lose all its grant, and so increase the burden on London ratepayers. To understand the rest of the story, the reader needs to take on board at least some of the rudimentary principles of the block grant system.

Its central feature is an estimate made by Government of how much each individual council needs to spend to provide an average standard of service. That estimate is called the Grant Related Expenditure Assessment. (Heseltine used to abbreviate this to GREA, which he pronounced as in Germaine Greer. Almost everyone else spells out the initials GRE.)

The GREs have no connection with the amount councils may have spent in the past. They attempt to measure how much each local authority needs to spend on the basis of elaborate computer analysis of its characteristics, such as its numbers of old people and children, the length of its roads and the extent of its overcrowded housing.

Under Heseltine's system, if a council spent at GRE, its ratepayers would pay no more than a standard (national average) rate. The Government would provide enough grant to make up the difference between the council's income from this 'standard' rate and the cost of providing the 'standard' level of services. But if a council spent substantially more than its GRE, the ratepayers would be made to pay an increasing proportion of the burden. For authorities like the GLC which were rich in rateable resources, extra spending would bring an actual cut in grant. So GLC ratepayers would not only have to find the entire cost of any additional items in the budget. They would also have to pay for the grant which had been forfeited.

Michael Heseltine takes cover, December 16, 1980 (*Press Association*)

The new system was profoundly disturbing for people who prized local autonomy. It provided the Government with a power-ful lever to influence the traditional relationship between council-lors and their electors. Given a few years, it is possible that block grant would have delivered Heseltine's objective by encouraging councils to spend closer to their GREs. The ink was hardly dry on the legislation, however, before Heseltine realised that its im-mediate effect would be counter-productive. Low-spending councils were likely to increase their budgets towards the standard faster than the high spenders could be induced to cut. Heseltine's political division of councils into 'goodies' and 'baddies' was in danger of sabotaging the economic objective of reducing expendi-ture.

Heseltine was under considerable pressure to deliver cuts in a hurry. The previous Labour Government had planned for local government spending to increase by 3 per cent between 1978/9 and 1980/1; but the new Thatcher administration replaced this with a 2 per cent cut. In November 1980 Sir Geoffrey Howe, the Chancellor, announced an additional 3 per cent cut for 1981/2. The Cabinet wanted local government squeezed hard and fast.

So in January 1981, Heseltine announced a set of specific spending targets for local authorities which bore no relation to their GREs. Each council was told to spend 5.6 per cent less in real terms in 1981/2 than it had in 1978/9. High spenders and low spenders were treated the same.

This exhortation did not work. When the councils sent in their budget returns in the spring of 1981, Heseltine found that they were planning to overspend his targets by £800 million (5 per cent). In June 1981 he called for revised budgets and warned that councils failing to make the necessary cuts would be penalised by means of a grant fine which was nicknamed 'holdback'. So an authority like the GLC faced a double disincentive to overspend. If it spent substantially over its GRE it would lose grant anyway under the ordinary block grant mechanism. If it spent over target, it would be additionally penalised by holdback.

This was the quickly-changing financial environment in which the Livingstone administration started work in May 1981. The full rigour of the new grant system was not known when the manifesto was drawn up, but Labour members had no intention of allowing it to blow them off course. The main plank of their election manifesto had been to cut LT fares by 25 per cent and freeze them at that level thereafter. They planned to make the cut in October, half-way through the GLC financial year.

The cost of this commitment had been carefully worked out by Andrew McIntosh before he led Labour into the May elections. He realised that the Cutler administration had set a budget for 1981/2 which provided insufficient subsidies for LT to get through the year without a round of fare increases. Labour therefore had to cover that deficit and compensate LT for the proposed cuts in fares and increases in services. The cost was expected to be about £100 million during the 1981/2 financial year, which would be raised by levying a supplementary rate of 5p in the pound. Londoners were warned about this before they voted Labour into office.

Heseltine's grant system destroyed that relatively simple arithmetic. In spite of Cutler's efforts to keep spending and rate increases down ahead of the elections, his GLC budget of £456 million was already £50 million above its GRE. Any extra spending therefore would cause the GLC to lose grant under the new block grant system. Heseltine's holdback penalties against councils failing to make the 5.6 per cent cuts would take further grant away. Together these measures almost doubled the cost to ratepayers of Labour's cheap fares programme.

Far from backtracking, the Livingstone administration decided to increase the cost of the fares cuts. When the LT chairman, Sir Peter Masefield, presented his proposals for implementing the 25 per cent fares reduction, many members of the Labour group were appalled to find that their constituents could end up facing fare increases. The manifesto had envisaged reorganising the LT fare structure into a simplified zonal system. Masefield's proposals gave big fare reductions to Underground commuters to the outer London suburbs, but many bus passengers and people travelling on short Underground journeys in inner London would have had to pay slightly more. As Livingstone puts it: 'If you'd

"Are you spending £¼ million to explain why you're putting £100 million on the rates, or £100 million to explain why you're putting £¼ million on the rates?" *Standard*, February 9, 1983 (*Jak*)

actually designed it to clobber Labour voters, you couldn't have done it better.' So, under pressure from inner London councillors, the group decided to 'top up' the original commitment to produce a zonal system with no losers. That raised the average fares reduction from 25 per cent to 32 per cent and increased the cost of the package to £117.3 million.

At that level of extra spending the GLC lost £111 million of the £122 million grant for which Cutler had budgeted. The total burden on ratepayers became £228.3 million and the supplementary rate necessary to pay for it increased to 11.9 pence in the pound. The cost of this supplementary bill to the average London household was £1.31 per week from October until March. This more than doubled Londoners' weekly outgoings to the GLC in the second half of the financial year. (Ratepayers in inner London were also presented with a 3.2 pence in the pound supplementary education rate from ILEA.)

It should be remembered that these sums of money represented only a small proportion of what people paid for their local government services. GLC and ILEA rate precepts are passed on to the boroughs for collection along with their own rate and a rate for the Metropolitan Police. Even after the cheap fares policy was introduced, the GLC rate formed less than a fifth of the average Londoner's 1981/2 rate bill. And, in spite of the GLC's loss of grant, the financial benefit which the average London household was to get from cheap fares was greater than the addition to its rates. The exercise produced some transfer of benefit in favour of people who used public transport, but that was one of its main purposes – to encourage people to leave their cars at home and relieve London's congestion. The real cost of the exercise fell on London's businesses, which paid 61 per cent of the GLC rate. Even they benefited when cheap fares reduced their employees' need for pay increases and relieved congestion for transporting their goods. They ended up subsidising the public transport system less than their counterparts in Paris under its right-wing Gaullist mayor, Jacques Chirac.

The cheap fares experiment was not the product of some eccentric extravagance of London's outside left. It was modelled on a fare freeze which had been maintained by South Yorkshire metropolitan county council since 1975. The Labour groups which had swept to power in all the metropolitan counties in the May 1981 elections all had some form of cheaper fares commitment following a concordat, arranged with the help of the Shadow Transport Secretary, Albert Booth, at Labour's local government conference in Blackpool in February 1981.

Even when it became clear that cuts in Government grant would make the cost of cheaper fares in London much greater than expected, there was no suggestion from the GLC Labour right that the 25 per cent fares cut should not go ahead. McIntosh's only criticism of Livingstone is that he 'hadn't got the guts' to resist the pressure from inner London members which turned the 25 per cent package into 32 per cent. But this was only a relatively minor item in financial terms. London's cheap fares initiative, which came to be known as 'Fares Fair', was perceived by Labour as a moderate and mainstream policy.

That is not how it looked to Heseltine. From his perspective the GLC and metropolitan counties were completely wrecking his chances of delivering the public spending target. He had a reasonable response to the call he had made for councils to revise their budgets. Of the 413 English authorities, 257 offered to make cuts worth £196 million. But a handful of councils sent in revised budgets which increased their spending by £211 million. The net result was that the total overspend increased to £815 million. Heseltine was made to look foolish and he had no doubts about where to pin the blame. The GLC, West Midlands and Mersey-side had together increased their original budgets by £167 million to pay for cheaper fares. Heseltine became convinced that his efforts to curb council spending were being thwarted by a tiny number of 'extremist' Labour councils whose 'overspending' had to be curbed by more direct action. The GLC was top of his hit list.

During the summer of 1981 the DoE prepared new legislation designed to isolate the high spenders. Heseltine was still unwilling to take outright control of individual council budgets, as his colleague George Younger, Secretary of State for Scotland, was doing north of the border (where the rebel Lothian council was beaten into submission). He recognised that England had stronger traditions of local independence. Its greater population size and sheer number of local authorities also made it harder to manage centrally. So Heseltine developed an ingenious compromise designed to allow him to impose his will on individual high-spending councils without having the constitutional and administrative problems of full control.

On November 6, 1981, he brought before Parliament a new Local Government Finance Bill. Under this, all local authorities would remain responsible for fixing their main rate demand in the spring, but they would only be allowed to finance up to a level of spending which was acceptable to the Government. Any authority wanting to spend more would be made to ask for a supplementary rate in June. Businesses were to be at least partially protected from this supplementary. So the burden of extra spending would be cast disproportionately on to domestic ratepayers. Moreover, councils would not be allowed to levy the supplementary unless they won support for it in a referendum of their local electors. If the voters said no, the councils would be forced to ask the Government to bail them out with a loan. The strings attached to this loan would be tantamount to spending controls by Whitehall.

The strategy was cunning. It allowed Heseltine to argue that he was not centralising power, but merely giving it to the people. Voters would be able to choose in the referendum whether they wanted high-spending or not. Yet the Government was dealing itself all the winning cards. It would decide the spending level at which the referendum trap would be sprung so as to pick off a handful of councils spending well above their GRE. Extra spending would fall primarily on domestic ratepayers who would also have to fund their councils' loss of grants. The Government propaganda machine would be set in motion to persuade people that the extra spending was profligate. It was almost inconceivable that the electors would vote to pay supplementary rates.

Although the referendum legislation did not spell out the arithmetic of the scheme, there was no doubt that Heseltine intended the GLC and ILEA to fall into the trap. His proposals made it look impossible for the GLC Labour group to get through the next year with its manifesto commitments intact. To avoid the referendum, the GLC would probably have had to raise fares and rents, scrap its industry programme and abandon every item of budgetary growth promised to the electorate in May. To keep to the manifesto, it would probably have had to treble or quadruple the domestic rate. There was no chance that this would have been approved in a referendum.

Local Labour politicians had never faced such a challenge to their principles and integrity. As the Heseltine plan emerged in a series of leaks and statements between July and November, GLC Labour councillors began to realise that they would have to choose between surrender to the Government's call for cuts, resignation, or tactics of confrontation and defiance.

It was the critical nature of this impending clash which made Livingstone's colleagues so angry about his media profile at the time. His extra-mural statements on Ireland and other issues distracted attention from the worst crisis Labour local government had ever faced.

Livingstone's own view on the crisis was spelt out in a front-page leading article in *Labour Herald*, a socialist weekly paper set up by Livingstone, Ted Knight (leader of Lambeth council) and Matthew Warburton in September 1981 'to act as a forum for the preparation of a fightback in local government'. On October 16 they wrote:

Legislation proposed by the Environment Secretary, Michael Heseltine, to take control of local government finance, places Labour controlled councils in a new and intolerable situation.

The manifestos which won Labour control of all the metropolitan counties and many county councils in May were drawn up on the basis that the community as a whole, including industry and commerce, should contribute to the cost of providing services.

The basis of this is to be invalidated by a single Act of Parliament. There is no way in which Labour councils can balance the books under the proposed new system without either making impossible cuts or domestic rate increases.

Labour councils must refuse to vote for cuts in services or rent and fare increases. But they must also refuse to vote for rate increases under the Tories' new system.

This argument for no cuts and no rate increases involved a breach of councils' obligations to balance their books. It had been advanced by hard-left supporters of Socialist Organiser at previous budget-fixing seasons; but it had never been implemented. It was clearly illegal, a tactic designed to bring confrontation with the Government to a head. *Labour Herald* explained:

There will be comrades who will argue that we should resign from councils, let the Tories make the cuts and boycott the resulting by-elections or contest them on the basis that we will refuse to take our seats.

Such a course would be completely wrong. It would leave the workers in each council exposed to massive attacks because they cannot run away from their jobs. Ordinary families in the community would never understand why the Labour council failed to defend them and left them to resist the cuts alone.

Labour councils must stay and fight ... We should merge our campaigns for the restoration of government grant with our opposition to the new legislation by imposing a full rates freeze in next year's budget and voting down any proposal from the Tories to cut ...

The scene was therefore set for confrontation. It remained extremely unlikely that Livingstone would win sufficient support from his Labour group to carry an illegally unbalanced budget at the ratemaking meeting in February 1982. But, whether he did or not, it seemed impossible for Labour to stay in office implementing its manifesto promises. The GLC Labour group was to be put on the rack and stretched to breaking point.

Two events in the second week of November then totally transformed the position. On November 10 Lord Denning and two fellow Appeal Court judges declared that the GLC's cheap fares, which had been introduced a month before, were illegal. This set off the train of events which was to force a doubling of fares in the following March. And on November 12, Heseltine was forced to withdraw his Local Government Finance Bill because of opposition by Tory backbenchers. Few Tory MPs were concerned about its threat to local government independence and most would have relished the embarrassment it would have caused Livingstone. Heseltine's bill was killed because a lot of Tories did not like the principle of referendums becoming an established part of British politics.

The story of how the courts outlawed the cheap fares policy will be pursued in the next chapter. Its result was that the GLC Labour group was eventually forced to jettison a manifesto commitment which was becoming financially too expensive to afford, but politically too important to give up.

Heseltine attempted to salvage his position after the embarrassing setback in the Commons by introducing a Local Government Finance (No 2) Bill. But this lacked the clout of his original version. It would have been possible for Heseltine simply to have dropped the offending referendum clause. If Labour councils had been forced to finance 'excessive' spending through unpopular

Livingstone and Deputy Leader Illtyd Harrington present Mrs Thatcher with a bill for London's lost grant, April 18, 1983 (*Popperfoto*)

supplementary rates, many would have felt obliged to make the cuts which Ministers wanted, even without the immediate discipline of a referendum. Instead Heseltine scrapped the whole system and introduced a new clause to ban supplementary rates. This had virtually no effect on the subsequent 'overspending' problem. Over the next two years the Government was repeatedly to relax local authority spending targets to make the total more realistic. It also made the grant penalties for overspending more severe. But by the end of the first Thatcher administration in June 1983, English councils were spending marginally more than in May 1979. Collectively, in real terms, they had cut nothing but their plans for growth.

Efforts to find an alternative to domestic rates as a source of local government finance also met with no success. Faced with this record of failure, the Government approached the 1983 general election with the need to pledge firm action. If Heseltine had not lost his referendum bill, it is most unlikely that the 1983 Conservative manifesto would have needed to contain the promise to control excessive council spending by force of law. Nor would it have called for the abolition of the GLC and metropolitan counties.

The conclusion we are left with from this episode in the Livingstone story is that the fates were very kind to him. After only six months in office, his administration appeared to be in an appalling mess. Even if the referendum legislation had never been conceived, the GLC Labour programme was under severe financial strain. Through the summer and autumn of 1981, the Labour leaders of the London boroughs had been putting pressure on Livingstone to keep the next GLC rate increase, due in April 1982, as low as possible. They argued that a big rate demand would destroy Labour's chances in the four-yearly borough elections in May. But the cost of the Fares Fair commitment made it inevitable that the GLC rate would soar.

The nearest that Livingstone got to a compromise on this issue was in a preliminary draft budget which won a two-thirds majority in the Labour group on November 2. This pretended the referendum legislation did not exist. It honoured the fares pledge, but left almost no room for other manifesto initiatives. In spite of this sacrifice, the rate increase would have been 124 per cent compared with Cutler's 1981 budget. It cannot be assumed that the Labour right, under pressure from their friends in the boroughs, would eventually have accepted this increase; nor that the Labour left would have agreed to sacrifice so many non-transport items from the programme.

The judgment from the Labour chief whip of the time, Harvey Hinds, is that he would have had a very hard job mobilising a majority in council for the 1982 budget. 'The cumulative effect had we been allowed to carry out all our policies would have been such that there would have been a rebellion in the Labour group against the consequential rate precept increase,' he says. And if the leadership had decided to jettison manifesto promises? 'This would have created the most enormous political row in the Labour group and in the Labour Party in London. It could well have brought down the administration.'

These were the sort of internal tensions which broke the unity of the Goodwin GLC administration in 1975. There is no way of telling how Livingstone would have coped with a similar crisis when it came, perhaps in 1982, perhaps in 1983. But on the evidence of these last two chapters, he was in pretty poor shape.

Livingstone's problems were not limited to finance and the media. During his first six months in office, the GLC Labour group suffered a series of punishing reverses on several of the main pledges which had been made in the election campaign. For left-wingers who prided themselves on a superior ability to adhere to a manifesto, these setbacks were hard to stomach. A promise that ILEA would cut the price of school meals from 35p to 25p was overturned following legal advice that councillors could be sur-charged and disqualified from public office. Although a majority of the Labour group had voted to go ahead in spite of the surcharge threat, they could not carry enough members with them to carry the vote in the full ILEA council.

Legal difficulties were also associated with failure to fulfil manifesto ambitions to stop the transfer of GLC-owned housing to the London boroughs. Housing management had once been one of the GLC's main functions, enabling it to take important decisions on rents, the allocation of tenancies, estate modernisa-tion and repairs. This role was deliberately run down by the Cutler administration which argued that public housing could be run more responsively at borough level and that London did not have the problems of housing shortage which required strategic GLC intervention. By 1981 Cutler had transferred GLC estates in most of London to borough management and was preparing to com-plete the process in the remaining inner boroughs.

GLC lawyers informally advised the Labour group six months before the election that a Labour GLC could effectively resist further transfers. By May 1981, however, the Government had sewn the matter up in a rock-hard statutory instrument which the new Labour group was told it was powerless to challenge.

A second important strand of Labour housing policy was to stop

"Can you afford to keep my daughter *and* Ken Livingstone?" *Standard*, October 29, 1981 (*Michael Heath*)

the voluntary sale of GLC housing to private individuals. Attempts to abort contracts which the Tory administration had already signed with aspiring purchasers of GLC properties in Hammersmith foundered in a lost court case. The Labour group's attempt to revive the GLC's housing investment role from the minuscule level of only thirty-five starts throughout London in 1980/1 was also kyboshed by the Government when Heseltine vetoed GLC proposals for a £200 million annual programme to achieve 1,500 starts a year. Although Gladys Dimson as housing chair had direct responsibility for this area of policy, Livingstone (whose original local government interest had been housing) spent a large part of his time in the early months on these housing battles, almost all of which ended in defeats at the hands of the superior forces of Government and the law.

Perhaps even more disturbing were the setbacks to Labour's industry and employment policy, the most innovative part of its manifesto. This programme envisaged setting up a Greater London Enterprise Board which would use funds provided by the council, its workers' pension fund and the financial markets to invest in the industrial regeneration of London.

'We discovered that without our permission or knowledge, the officers had rushed off to get a legal opinion from someone who was bound to be damning,' says Livingstone. 'Mike Ward [the industry committee chair] then had to spend months overriding that opinion with other legal advice to get round it.'

Livingstone maintains that many of these early reverses were the result of obstructiveness by the GLC bureaucracy. 'What the officers realised was that, given our narrow majority, any legal opinion saying we were at risk of surcharge meant they could block what we wanted to do. They rushed off to get the school meals opinion without our being involved. They rushed off to get the GLEB opinion without members' knowledge . . .

'We discovered that there had been a tradition in the building that whenever there was a Labour administration, the officers went to known Conservative barristers for opinions; and when there was a Tory administration they went to known Labour barristers – just to be safe. No large corporation in this country ever goes to a barrister and asks for an academic exercise about his view of the law. They go and say: we want to do this, find us a justification.' GLC officers deny such allegations of deliberate obstructiveness. They argue that local authorities, unlike companies, often need to take a legal opinion to demonstrate that they care about the law.

Nevertheless by June 1981 the Labour administration had taken steps to behave more like these large corporations. A procedure was established that no officer could seek a legal opinion without the permission of the ruling policy committee or, if necessary, the leader himself. The GLC's panel of barrister advisers was also 'balanced up' with people of 'a more radical turn of mind'. That produced a flow of much more favourable opinions.

The one area of the manifesto where such legal gamesmanship seemed unnecessary was the cheap fares policy. At no stage did anyone even contemplate that Fares Fair might be illegal. Neither the GLC's politicians, nor its officers, doubted that the council had the statutory discretion to implement Fares Fair. Nor did anyone imagine that the courts would find it unreasonable for the GLC to implement a major policy commitment which had been put before the electorate. These presumptions were shattered in one of the most sensational court defeats that a local authority has ever experienced.

7 · Vandals in Ermine

The legal challenge which was to destroy the GLC's transport policy was set in motion one Sunday lunchtime at the Bird in Hand public house in Gravel Road, Bromley. Dennis Barkway, Tory leader of Bromley borough council, was having his regular weekend drink with three political colleagues: Fred David and Philip Jones, his fellow ward councillors; and Simon Randall, former leader of Bromley and one of its GLC members.

These sessions were designed to give them a chance to chat sociably about the affairs of their borough, a well-heeled commuter area to the south-east of the metropolis. But, as in so many pubs across London that Sunday, the conversation did not take long to get round to the latest exploits of 'Red Ken'. Wasn't his supplementary rate demand disgraceful? One more nail in the coffin of London's industry and commerce . . . It was unfair to people in Bromley who lived miles from the nearest Underground station: they'd have to pay more rates without getting the full cheap fares benefit. What about the stockbrokers commuting in from Kent and Surrey? No extra rates for them, but they'd get the cheap fares when they reached central London . . . And the tourists! Why should foreigners on holiday be subsidised by the citizens of Bromley? It wasn't as if overseas travel agents said: visit London and save 10p on a bus ride.

This was the period in July 1981 when the press campaign against Livingstone was at its peak. Barkway now acknowledges that if it hadn't been for the outrage caused by Livingstone's media persona, the conversation at the Bird in Hand might not have developed as it did. Perhaps if Andrew McIntosh had been GLC leader, he might have realised the need to trim back the supplementary rate demand ('untrue,' says McIntosh). Perhaps if Livingstone had not gone on so much about Ireland, gays and the Royal Family, it might have been easier to knuckle under and pay the wretched rate. At all events the four councillors began to ask themselves whether the GLC's cheap fares policy was legal.

Surely, they mused, councillors had a legal obligation to act reasonably. Anything more unreasonable than this supplementary rate demand was hard, they thought, to imagine. And so Barkway, buoyed up by nothing more than his usual pint of lemonade, resolved to act. He consulted the Bromley council solicitor, Richard Pugh, who agreed there might be the basis for a legal challenge. With permission from the Tory group, they asked for an opinion from counsel which supported Pugh's assessment that the GLC might not only have been unreasonable but might also have adopted illegally hasty procedures.

The affair could easily have proceeded no further. Court action was going to be expensive and, as Barkway puts it, Bromley is not exactly a pioneering authority when it comes to spending the public's money. Part of the group wanted to hang fire until other boroughs could be brought in to share the cost. But Barkway reasoned that it could take months for the necessary approvals to pass through the cycles of countless committees. He persuaded the Bromley Tories to press ahead on the assumption that other Tory boroughs would join in later with financial backing.

In fact Bromley never got that support. Barkway recalls one letter from Peter Bowness, Tory leader of Croydon and chairman of the London Boroughs Association, warning that the action hadn't got a snowball's chance in hell. 'All the punchy Conservative boroughs were turning out to be not so punchy when it came to putting money up.'

The purpose of this small detour into south London suburban politics is to stress the lack of inevitability of the GLC's defeat in the courts. Most people thought the Bromley Tories were off their heads. Until that point it had been assumed that the GLC was perfectly within its rights to decide on policy grounds to subsidise London Transport (LT) by 'reasonable' amounts. The Transport (London) Act 1969 had placed a duty on the GLC to promote 'integrated, efficient and economic transport facilities for Greater London' (section 1). It had also given the GLC power to make grants to the LT Executive 'for any purpose' (section 3).

During its second reading in the House of Commons, the then Transport Minister Richard (now Lord) Marsh said: 'The main powers that the [GLC] Council will have, apart from the power to appoint, will be to pay grant to the Executive for any purpose it thinks fit and to issue directions to the Executive. This gives the Council the right to prescribe the policy lines to be followed and to take financial responsibility for its decisions. This is very important, because if the Council wishes the Executive to do something that will cause it to fall short of its financial targets, it will itself have to take financial responsibility for it. The Council might wish, for example, the Executive to run a series of services at a loss for social or planning reasons. It might wish to keep fares down at a time when costs are rising and there is no scope for economies. It is free to do so. But it has to bear the cost' (*Hansard*, 17.12.68, cols. 1247–8).

The courts are not allowed to pay any attention to such Ministerial statements to the House. They must concentrate on the actual words in Acts of Parliament. But, as far as the administrators at the GLC and LT were concerned, the Transport (London) Act said what Marsh intended it to say. They had no doubts about the GLC's power to pay grants to subsidise fares for social or planning reasons.

So when Bromley brought its case to the Divisional Court on October 28, 1981, the GLC side thought there would be no problem with Bromley's first submission: that the GLC lacked the power to order a fares cut. That left two other arguments. Was the amount spent on the Fares Fair policy reasonable, bearing in mind a council's general duty to look after the interests of its ratepayers? And did the GLC go through the correct procedures before it reached its decision?

Lord Justice Dunn and Mr Justice Phillips decided all points in favour of the GLC. On November 3 they dismissed, with costs, Bromley's application that the supplementary rate should be quashed. They rejected arguments put by Bromley's counsel, David Widdicombe QC, that the Transport (London) Act required the GLC to run the transport system as a business venture, observing that even Widdicombe conceded LT could not be run at a profit. It was, they said, a matter of discretion how much subsidy should be given and the Act gave the discretion to the GLC, provided the council exercised it after fully considering 'all the relevant factors'.

Both judges thought that the complete abolition of fares would not have been legal. Mr Justice Phillips even ventured to suggest that the Fares Fair plan lay on the margin of what was permissible; but he said it did not go over the edge into being unlawful. The judges also rejected Widdicombe's contention that the GLC had failed to go through the correct procedures in reaching its decision. The council was deemed to have considered all the pros and cons, including the cost to the ratepayers.

At this stage the Bromley councillors nearly gave up. A committee of five members, including Barkway, set up to handle the case, gathered solemnly at Bromley civic centre expecting to be advised to throw in the towel. Instead they were told by the council solicitor, Pugh, that an appeal was likely to succeed. The lower court judges had failed to deal with some important points of law, he said; and they had been reluctant to make a judgment which could be deemed 'political' by challenging the GLC's use of its discretion. The professional advice was to appeal, with the proviso that if Bromley lost it could face a legal bill of up to £200,000. After an hour of strained debate, Barkway recommended that the official's advice should be accepted. The appeal was under way.

Back at County Hall, Livingstone was hearing similar interpretations from the GLC lawyers, who were by no means happy about the points of law which had been exposed in the lower court. They expected Bromley to go to the Appeal Court and they feared the GLC might lose.

The case was swiftly heard by the Master of the Rolls, Lord Denning, sitting with Lord Justice Oliver and Lord Justice Watkins. On November 10 they unanimously declared that the fares cut and the supplementary rate were unlawful. The most vigorously damning judgment came from Oliver, who demolished the GLC's presumption that it had clear powers to subsidise LT.

Oliver found a clause in the Act which produced a completely different interpretation. Section 7 (3) says that the LT Executive has a duty to balance its books 'as far as practicable'. Now the administrators had thought this merely meant that LT should strive to avoid making a deficit after taking account of the money it had been promised from the GLC by way of grant. They thought the clause was designed to ensure that the LT Executive met the financial objectives which the GLC had set. Oliver disagreed. He saw section 7 (3) as an overriding obligation on the Executive to run its affairs on ordinary business lines. The Fares Fair experiment had been a clear breach of the businesslike principle, he said.

This was a devastating judgment. The GLC Labour group was by then almost resigned to being picked up on some procedural technicality. Indeed Oliver went on to rule that the fare cut was also unlawful because the GLC had not given direction to LT 'in writing'. But if the fault had been merely procedural, it could probably have been remedied by making sure that similar policies were put through the council and implemented in the correct manner. Oliver's ruling destroyed the assumptions on which everyone, including the Transport Secretary and two High Court judges, had been operating. He denied the GLC's statutory power to choose to run LT at a deficit in the interests of Londoners.

On its own Oliver's ruling would have been hard enough for the GLC Labour group to swallow. Denning and Watkins, however, produced concurring judgments larded with gratuitous comments of such political insensitivity that the question of their legal merits was obscured in the ensuing public debate.

Denning said that the majority on the GLC had decided to honour their election manifesto 'come what may', even after they had been told that it would injure ratepayers far more seriously than they had originally realised (before Heseltine's grant penalties were invoked). A manifesto issued by a political party in order to get votes was not to be regarded as a gospel. It was not a covenant, Denning said. 'Many electors did not vote for the manifesto, they voted for the party. When a party was returned to power, it should consider what it was best to do, and what was practical and fair.'

Watkins said that the council's decision arose out of a hasty,

Livingstone and Transport Chairman Dave Wetzel make a point (*GLC*)

unlawful and arbitrary use of power. 'Gladstone has said that power was the true test of a man or a class or a people. Just after the election the Leader of the GLC had sought out Sir Peter Masefield [chairman of LT] and said that the GLC intended forthwith to put their fares policy into effect. He was talking in a position of strength to a chairman who seemed to have no authority. It was a bad case of an abuse of power, which totally disregarded the interests of the ratepayers.'

Their observations caused apoplexy on the left and were the foundation of much of the popular support for the GLC which followed. The whole struggle of the Labour left had been to shape the internal mechanisms of the party to ensure that elected representatives and leaders carried out manifesto policies. Here was 82-year-old Lord Denning suggesting that the first thing an elected council should do on assuming office was to put its manifesto on one side and consider 'what it was best to do'. Here was Lord Justice Watkins disapproving of Livingstone's 'abuse of power' in giving directions to the GLC appointee who ran LT to prepare options for the council. If there had been a single policy which got through to the electorate in May 1981, it had been Labour's commitment to cut fares. What right had unelected judges to flout the will of the people?

The point that Denning and Watkins were getting at was that, under existing law, councillors (unlike MPs) are bound to go through certain approved motions in reaching their decisions. They must demonstrate the reasonableness of their actions partly by showing that they have accumulated and studied relevant data before they do anything. This does not mean they are expected to shred their manifestos on gaining power. The reasons which persuaded them to draw up a manifesto will usually be quite good enough to allow them to implement it. But, legally, the semblance of open-mindedness must be maintained.

In reality this law is a nonsense. In the months that followed GLC councillors were heard time and again going through an approved litany in the council chamber along the lines that they had 'taken all relevant factors into account' and had 'ignored all irrelevant factors'. Such charades do not improve the quality of decisions. Nor, often, does time and money spent shopping around for opinions from counsel to justify preconceived policies. As the law stands, however, Denning's criticism of the haste with which the Fares Fair plan was implemented might have been somewhat less unacceptable if he had not wrapped it up in such extraordinarily inflammatory language.

A word of explanation may also be helpful on Oliver's more fundamental criticism that the GLC had no authority to cut the fares even if it had gone through the correct procedures in making its decision. Under British law, local authorities only have power to act in ways which are specifically permitted by Parliament (except for the minor power to spend a 2p rate more or less as they choose). Electoral support provides councils with no additional source of legitimacy. If a party had won the GLC elections pledged for example to introduce a wealth tax to abolish poverty in London, it would have been clearly promising to act outside its legal powers. Popularity has nothing to do with legality. The issue before the courts in this case was whether the GLC had made reasonable use of its powers to run the public transport system.

For their different reasons three Appeal Court judges said no. If they were right in their interpretation of the law, the only conclusion for supporters of Fares Fair was that the law was an ass, that the Transport (London) Act needed amendment and, perhaps, that councils should be given much broader powers to act in any way that the law did not specifically forbid.

But were they right? The GLC appealed to the House of Lords and appointed Robert Alexander QC to take over its case. Day by day GLC officials attending the hearing came back to County Hall convinced that Alexander was winning the argument on every salient point. 'We were always told that Denning would go berserk, but that the Law Lords would restore the damage,' says Livingstone. 'That wasn't just the view of our people. It was the view of those organs such as ITV and BBC who'd retained lawyers to watch the case to advise them on it. Everyone came back saying: you've won.

'At that stage we were told that we might just lose on a technicality to save Denning's face, but we'd be able to do it all properly and the fares would stay down. Therefore we were absolutely stunned to find that we lost on all the basic points of law. That's why we weren't geared up for the media campaign. We were completely unprepared.'

Five Law Lords unanimously ruled on December 17 that the GLC's cheap fares policy and the supplementary rate which funded it were unlawful. Four of them, Lord Wilberforce, Lord Keith, Lord Scarman and Lord Brandon, accepted most of Oliver's statutory interpretation. They agreed that the GLC had failed to recognise an obligation that LT should break even 'as far as practicable'. As Scarman put it: 'It is plain that the 25 per cent overall [fares] reduction was adopted not because any higher fare level was impracticable, but as an object of social and transport policy. It was not a reluctant yielding to economic necessity, but a policy of preference. In doing so the GLC abandoned business principles. That was a breach of duty owed to the ratepayers and wrong in law.'

Lord Diplock disagreed. He accepted that the GLC could deliberately choose to subsidise LT in pursuit of its public transport policies. In his view Fares Fair was unlawful because it imposed an undue financial burden on London's ratepayers. He found it difficult to say whether the original package in the Labour manifesto would have been legally acceptable. That would have lowered fares by 25 per cent at a cost to ratepayers of £69 million. For Diplock the crucial point was that the extra fares subsidy caused the GLC to lose £50 million in grants under Heseltine's penalty system.

'The GLC's decision was not simply about allocating a total financial burden between passengers and ratepayers, it was also a decision to increase that total burden so as nearly to double it and to place the whole of the increase on the ratepayers.' Farepayers would get benefits worth £69 million while ratepayers would face costs worth £119 million.

'That would, in my view, clearly be a thriftless use of monies obtained by the GLC from ratepayers and a deliberate failure to deploy to the best advantage the full financial resources available to it by avoiding any action that would involve forfeiting grants from central government funds. It was thus a breach of the fiduciary duty owed by the GLC to the ratepayers.'

The great irony of this judgment was, as it later emerged, that Heseltine's grant penalties were themselves legally suspect. Legislation had to be put through Parliament in 1982 after Department of the Environment lawyers realised the Government lacked the power to penalise overspenders. In the end no penalties were invoked until this measure received Royal Assent.

Disproportionate attention is being given to Diplock's judgment because it has wider significance which may outlive the vagaries of the Transport (London) Act when that is repealed as part of the Government's new plans for LT. Diplock's emphasis on 'fiduciary duty' – the notion that councillors must behave rather like trustees of their ratepayers' money – became an important strand of the argument about local authorities' freedom to determine how their areas are administered. His point was supported in less trenchant terms by Wilberforce and Brandon and it was not gainsaid by the other two Law Lords. It opened up the suspicion among Labour groups throughout the country that the judiciary had given Heseltine's targets something closely akin to the force of law. Heseltine was in no hurry to disillusion them.

Livingstone is still convinced that the judiciary were politically motivated. 'All through the cases I'd been told it would be better for me not to go near the court, because my presence would upset the judges. The judges were just generally antagonistic to us. I now think that whatever case we'd ended up on in the Court of Appeal and the House of Lords, we would have lost. If we hadn't been done on the fares, I most probably would have been done on the Camden surcharge [see pp. 66–7]. I think it was the reaction against the judges on fares that most probably saved the Camden councillors because the judges at that stage had started to pull back.

'At the time we were advised that we had a very very good chance of winning in the House of Lords. When the names of the judges to hear the case were published, we were told that was good, because they were all the liberal judges. In retrospect we would have been better off with deeply conservative people in the legal sense of a strict constructionalist approach to the law. We had the misfortune, I think, to get five judges, four of whom liked to dabble in the classic American supreme court sense, to inter-pret the law in a political way.'

Misfortune or not, the GLC Labour group was faced just eight days before Christmas with the complete collapse of its central policy plank. The transport chairman, Dave Wetzel, condemned the Law Lords as 'Vandals in Ermine'. They had, he said, done more damage to public and private transport than any vandal does when he smashes a light on a bus or snaps an aerial on a car.

Livingstone summoned a press conference to warn that, unless the Government rushed through emergency legislation, the result of the judgment would be a 200 per cent increase in fares, cuts in services, the complete abandonment of some bus routes, closure of Underground stations and branch lines, and the loss of about a quarter of LT's 60,000 jobs.

In truth no one knew exactly what the judgment meant. The

Law Lords had said Fares Fair was illegal, but they had not said what level of fares subsidy would be legal. In a subsequent lecture to the Oxford University Faculty of Law, Maurice Stonefrost, GLC Comptroller of Finance, was asked if there was a 'fit' between the judgments and the administrative requirements for implementing them. He said there was, but only if you gave 'fit' its primary definition as 'a sudden seizure of hysteria, apoplexy, fainting, paralysis or epilepsy'. (Paper: An Administrator's viewpoint on R v GLC, ex p Bromley LBC, Stonefrost, March 2, 1983.) Livingstone's forecasts were based on an interpretation offered by his officers that it was illegal for LT to budget for a deficit.

Over at LT, Sir Peter Masefield suggested that a 150 per cent fare increase might be enough to keep within the law. Masefield's advisers thought it was sufficient to reverse the October fares cut, allow for inflation in 1981 and 1982 and make some contribution towards making up the illegal deficit of £120 million which would have been run up before fares could be increased in March.

Meanwhile the Transport Secretary, David Howell, was claiming that the fares need rise by only 60 per cent. He argued that all the GLC had to do was to restore the status quo of the original Cutler budget for 1981/2 by reversing the October fares cut and allowing for one year's inflation.

It was generally assumed at the time that both Livingstone and Howell were plucking figures out of the air to suit their political convenience. Howell's interest was to demonstrate that the whole mess was the fault of Livingstone and the loony left; he did not find palatable the idea that nice old Sir Horace might have been happily breaking the law for years with his modest dollops of subsidy. Livingstone's interest was to demoinstrate that the Law Lords' decision would produce mayhem in the streets of London as people took to their cars to avoid absurdly high bus and tube fares; he wanted to force the Government to sort out the problem by legislation to restore the GLC to the position everyone had believed pertained before Denning's judgment on November 10.

Livingstone was, however, being advised by counsel and

officers who had sat through the House of Lords hearings and had watched as each of the GLC's arguments that it was legally unnecessary for LT to break even was rejected. Their paramount concern was to produce a solution to an administrative problem which would be immune from further challenge. By December 23 the officers had prepared an even more gloomy interpretation of the judgments. A trebling of fares would be insufficient to maximise GLC revenues, they said. And the GLC would have to abandon concessionary off-peak fares for pensioners. On that day too, Larry Smith, Transport and General Workers Union national executive officer, warned of plans for a combined Underground and bus strike in protest at the Law Lords ruling. If it lasted more than a day London would seize up 'like a glue pot', he said.

At this stage the political tensions which were nearly to break the GLC Labour group apart had not yet surfaced. Members united behind the call for Government action to overrule the House of Lords judgment and they began to enjoy the first sustained bout of supportive media coverage about the wisdom of the cheap fares policy.

But after the holiday the divisions opened. On the right of the Labour group there were councillors who were terrified of the risk of surcharge – that they could be made to pay out of their own pockets for the £125 million deficit created by Fares Fair. Needless to say, the Labour group did not have this kind of money, but they feared complete personal bankruptcy and disqualification from office. GLC lawyers tried to convince them that it would be impossible to sustain a surcharge action for what had already been done. Since two High Court judges in the original Bromley hearings had thought the fares cuts reasonable, no one could say the policy was so unreasonable that no reasonable councillor could have supported it – the central test in any surcharge action. There was a real risk, however, that failure to comply with the Law Lords' ruling in future would be a surchargeable offence. This added to the right's natural inclination to ensure that the law must be obeyed.

On the left wing, quite a different argument was fomenting.

There the Law Lords' judgment seemed to be the final straw after a string of reverses, including the failure to cut school meal charges and to halt the transfer of estates to London boroughs. What, they asked, was the point of remaining in control of a council which was thwarted in all its key objectives? Should not the Labour group all resign or go into majority opposition? If the council was legally obliged to carry out Tory policies, let Tory councillors do their own dirty work.

This was similar to the argument which Livingstone himself had been advancing during the autumn in face of Heseltine's proposed new law to control local government spending through referendums. But now he put forward an entirely different strategy. Labour should stay in office, but refuse to put up the fares. It should defy the law and force the Government to intervene.

Even those of us who were close observers at County Hall at that time were never sure whether Livingstone seriously intended this illegal tactic to succeed. Many suspected that it was designed to preserve his left-wing credentials without sacrificing office. According to this cynical point of view, it was inevitable that no resolution recommending open defiance of the law would pass through the full GLC council. There would always be enough members of the Labour right and Opposition parties to defeat illegality. So, the cynics argued, Livingstone was playing a calculated political game. He wanted to appear defiant, but he also wanted to be beaten so that he could stay as leader of the GLC implementing the fare increases with the excuse that the manifesto had been betrayed not by him but by the votes of the Labour right.

Livingstone's own explanation of events is, however, equally plausible and, in showing how he wants to be remembered, it is a key item in his political make-up. To this we now turn.

'My first problem was to make sure the left didn't come to the conclusion that there was no point in carrying on . . . We were perceived (wrongly as it happens) as the first left administration anywhere. The last thing we could do was to fail. At the end of the day, if we were smashed and totally defeated, that was an acceptable end to the exercise. But to give up, or to take ourselves out of control when there was still something we could do, was not. It would immediately have painted the whole of the left for the foreseeable future as people who might win power but then might actually be unable to deliver, who might give up or disintegrate. And that was a stain which would be absolutely indelibly sloshed all over us by the right wing.'

Livingstone says he was supported in this by the attitude of the unions. 'They were determined that we should stay in office. We convened a meeting of all the transport unions. And the total advice of all of them was: you must be joking even thinking of resigning; we expect you to stay and fight because if you go out of office, there's going to be Tories running the show.'

But if resignation was unacceptable, so was implementing the Law Lords' ruling. 'My worry was that if we went ahead and voted for the fare increases and cuts in services, we would let the Government off the hook. Once we started to comply, they didn't need to do anything. I could see us getting in a position where we devastated the public transport system in London. The Government would have just sat back and crowed; and we would have ended up destroying ourselves as well as the public transport system.

'My guess was that if the council refused to comply with the Law Lords' judgment, the Government had to move. Either it had to take over and run the system itself, in which case it couldn't go along with devastating cuts, given that there were forty-nine Tory MPs in the London area. Or it would have had to back down and let us have the legislation we needed to run it as we wanted.'

So, as the GLC launched its public campaign in defence of Fares Fair (using £300,000 of ratepayers' money), Livingstone started to work on members of his group to persuade them that the line was defiance, not resignation.

Livingstone now acknowledges that defiance was not a sustainable long-term strategy. The GLC could not have passed a budget to pay for continuing Fares Fair – or, if it had, its rate demands would have had no legal status and it would have rapidly become bankrupt. He maintains, however, that the strategy was workable

in the short term. 'The only time you can effectively defy government is when you are being asked to do something and refuse to do
it. You can't defy government by taking a decision which actually is
illegal – because the officers here won't carry it out. But, if before
something can be done it requires the council to vote to do it
and the council fails to do it, then it can't happen. That was the
logic . . .

'Remember that the LT Executive had a degree of independence from us. They would have continued to pay the wages of the
staff. They would have continued to have fare revenue coming in.
They would have continued to have a level of subsidy coming from
the GLC. And they would have continued to borrow to pay the
difference . . . There was no way that Masefield was going to panic
and go berserk. He would have carried on running the system as
best he could until the Government did something. So by refusing
to comply, we actually would have put the ball back in the
Government's court.'

But what if the Government had allowed the GLC to stew in its
own illegality and deepening financial crisis?

'You would have reached a crunch within days. Remember the
coverage at the time – cameras, telly, everyone going berserk. Just
imagine, the largest council in the country, refusing to comply
with the law as laid down by Denning. It would have meant an
immediate constitutional crisis. The government couldn't have
waited for something to happen . . . It would have been the biggest
act of defiance against central government by a local authority
ever. It would have outdone Poplar or Clay Cross, because you
were talking about a third of a million pounds a day in illegal
spending. It would have been a major issue in Parliament. It would
have meant the Government had to do something quick.'

But surely it would have been impossibly humiliating for the
Government to change the legislation?

'Don't bank on that. Don't forget that when about a month later
you had the first vote on the Douglas Jay bill [Labour backbencher
proposing legalising cheap fares policy], twenty-five London
Tories managed not to be around. We won that vote. The
publicity campaign was starting to show that we had the majority of

the public on our side. MPs were being deluged with letters. There were huge public meetings, the biggest since the war in London. I'm not certain the government could have responded as it might have wanted to do.'

This then is the strategy which Livingstone took to the Labour group on January 11. By then, lawyers at the GLC and LT had sorted out the administrative problem of what the Law Lords' judgment meant. They put forward a package which would double fares on March 21, on the understanding that further increases of 50 to 100 per cent would be necessary later. Pensioners' bus passes were to be retained pending legislation promised by the Government to ensure their legality. But there were to be 15 per cent service cuts and other savings.

A resolution was due to go to the full GLC council on the following day, January 12, to implement this package. Livingstone's advice to his group was that they should vote against it. The group divided 23 votes to 22 in favour of Livingstone's recommendation and against compliance with the law.

They also decided by 22 votes to 20 that members should be allowed a free vote. The scene was set for a cliffhanger of a council meeting at which the rule of law was at risk.

Meanwhile in the Tory camp, Sir Horace Cutler was preparing a strategy which he believed would expose Labour's divisions as a shambles. The Tories believed that Livingstone's talk of doubling or trebling fares was pure scaremongering. They thought the GLC should take the advice of Transport Secretary Howell and make do with a 60 per cent increase – enough to restore the status quo of the original Tory budget in spring 1981 and allow a bit for inflation. So Cutler planned an amendment along these lines in the knowledge that Labour would unite to defeat it. Then the Tories could abstain on the main motion, leaving Labour split down the middle. The issue would have probably been decided by the three members of the SDP/Liberal Alliance who would have voted to stay within the law. Labour's embarrassment and confusion might even have forced the hated Livingstone to resign.

With this end in view, Cutler approached the council meeting in fine rumbustious form. From the Tory front bench he fulminated:

'If Mr Livingstone thinks that we are going to pull his hot chestnuts out of the fire so he can get off the griddle, then he has another think coming.' The Labour group was divided and the Conservatives were not going to let them off the hook, he said.

This Tory confidence didn't last for long. As soon as Cutler's amendment was put, his strategy was demolished by legal advice from the GLC director-general, Sir James Swaffield. In a frail voice the council's deputy chairman, Mrs Muriel Gumbel (a Tory), read out Swaffield's warning that any substantial departure from the officers' recommendation 'could mean that the council was in breach of its statutory duty and in contempt of court'. The Tories would themselves risk being surcharged for any additional costs that might arise.

No reliable estimates exist of the combined wealth on the Tory benches; but it can only be considered slight in relation to sums such as the LT deficit. The tremor of fear which swept across them was painful to behold.

The Conservatives were forced to submit a new legal amendment which 'reluctantly' recommended acceptance of the 100 per cent fares increase. They thought this was enough to keep them within the law. After Labour united to defeat this amendment, however, the Tories got another warning from Swaffield that abstention on the main vote might open them to surcharge if it resulted in the defeat of the officers' recommendation. By this stage it was becoming clear that Labour's majority for defying the law was hardening. Overnight Mike Ward, the industry committee chairman, switched his support behind the Livingstone strategy. That made the Labour split 24/21 in favour of illegality. There were three Alliance members. But would more Labour councillors change their minds to back the group decision?

The pressure on the Tories, who had come expecting to watch Labour squirm, was acute. Messages were passed in from wives and husbands in the members' restaurant beseeching spouses not to risk their property for a silly political principle.

In the end the Tories caved in – just enough. Three of their number went into the division lobby alongside 21 Labour and 3 Alliance members to provide a 27/24 victory for legality. The rest

Livingstone fails to rouse the rabble, Fares Fair debate, January 12, 1982 (*Guardian*)

fidgeted nervously doing head counts. The rule of law prevailed.

This Tory disarray thoroughly masked the collapse of Living-stone's stated strategy. It sustained the morale of the Labour group and Livingstone's own credibility as leader at a point of potential humiliation. There was much Conservative grumbling about Swaffield's role in their debacle, although most eventually recognised that he was only doing his job. If an official fails to warn members that their conduct may be surchargeable, he may himself be held liable for the cost. Normally such warnings would come at committee stage before business reaches full council, but in the circumstances of the Fares Fair chaos, no such opportunity arose. Livingstone had the luck and Cutler the embarrassment.

Are we to believe Livingstone's firm statement that he did want to win that vote and to embark on confrontation with the Government? In the confusion of the council meeting of January 12, it was impossible for him to know how the vote would go. To that extent he was prepared for confrontation if it came. He also worked hard to encourage members of his group to make the bravest decision of their lives and vote for defiance.

But some of those closest to him in the administration are convinced that he was bluffing. The deputy leader, Illtyd Harrington, who flew back from America on Concorde to attend the vital group meeting, says: 'This was the point when the moderates held the ground. There is no doubt in my mind that if we had voted not to give a direction to LT then we would have had a commissioner sent in and a major part of our executive function would have gone from us ... Some of us had to make decisions to obey the law to sustain the administration ... I think Ken was opportunistic because he knew that the law would have to be obeyed, but he knew other people would see to it that it was done. He was in a hell of a position: the darling of the left. He had no option but to vote with them. I understand that.'

Idealist or opportunist? The truth is probably less clear-cut. There were two possible outcomes on January 12: confrontation or compliance. Livingstone says he could have coped with confrontation. What he showed subsequently was that he lived with compliance. In a sense he never made the choice for himself. By its collective vote the GLC determined that Livingstone and his administration would head for respectability.

Like thousands of politicians before him, Livingstone decided that, since he could not do all that he wanted, he would do the most that he could. Under pressure, he moved towards a compromise with political reality.

It took the left a little while to follow suit. There was another serious split in the Labour group a fortnight later when the council was due to vote through LT's specific plans for implementing the fare increase. This time Livingstone voted with the right to accept the LT proposals on the grounds that further resistance would be merely a charade. 'There's a provision in the law which allows the

LT Executive to act in the absence of a firm direction from the GLC,' he says. 'Having told them initially that they must increase the fares, there was no way that they were not going to increase them simply because we couldn't agree on a particular form of words . . . The best approach was to minimise debate, just nod the thing through and concentrate on the campaign for changes in the legislation.'

But Livingstone failed to convince his colleagues of the need for this tactical switch. The left never met to discuss it. The group failed to debate it. And in a chaotic full meeting of the GLC council on January 26, the LT proposals were defeated by a coalition of the left and the Tories. The council degenerated into a political kindergarten in which a succession of twelve amendments were defeated amid an epidemic of standing-orderitis. 'God save London,' said the GLC deputy chairman, Charlie Rossi, as the proceedings neared their end. 'Every hour this debate goes on hastens the demise of the GLC. It is the most disgraceful display of a responsible body that I have ever seen,' said Andrew McIntosh. The whole occasion was pointless. LT went ahead anyway and raised the fares on March 21. 'An appalling mess,' Livingstone admits.

His behaviour during this episode infuriated councillors at the left end of the Labour group, who had been becoming increasingly disillusioned with his style of leadership over the previous eight months. The most vocal of them, John McDonnell, says that he arrived in County Hall after the election assuming that there would be a well-organised left majority which was ready for power. Instead he found the left caucus dominated by what he regarded as very centrist elements. He was appalled when in the first month Livingstone urged the group to oppose an LT workers' pay claim, mobilising the centre and the right to win the vote against about a dozen councillors on the left who said it should be conceded in full. 'I thought I was joining a left group and then all of a sudden we were on to these very middle-of-the-road policies and capitulating on a number of issues, as I saw it then,' says McDonnell.

The left stayed loyal in public for fear of opening a rift which could put the right-winger McIntosh back in control. But Living-stone's failure to maintain defiance against the Law Lords was the final straw. 'To go into court, lose and then have our own side voting in favour of the ruling, plus Livingstone as well in the second vote, was catastrophic, quite honestly. It destroyed the credentials of the leadership for the hard left within the Labour group for a long period of time.'

On January 29 some of the left councillors, including Mc-Donnell, Dave Wetzel and Valerie Wise, started the Can't Pay Won't Pay campaign to encourage illegal resistance to the fare increases. They urged passengers to refuse to pay the extra after the fares went up and to give the conductor or ticket collector a 'promise-to-pay' slip containing their names and addresses. This would explain that their action was a protest against the increases enforced by the Law Lords' ruling and that there was no intent to defraud. Can't Pay Won't Pay never became a mass campaign. Dave Wetzel, among others, ended up in Lavender Hill magis-trates' court where he was found guilty of fare-dodging. During the proceedings the magistrate criticised him for making chim-panzee-like gestures.

Meanwhile Livingstone was insisting that all Labour's efforts should be channelled into the council's official Keep Fares Fair campaign to change the law. By then he had also received a letter from sympathetic planners at Labour-controlled Camden council advising that, if the fares went up and services were cut, they could take court action against the GLC for failing to provide an efficient transport system. (This argument became the basis of the subsequent strategy for getting round the Law Lords' judgment and cutting fares again in 1983.)

Livingstone's official campaign achieved great success in win-ning the argument for cheap fares. In the public debate he ran rings round the faltering Transport Secretary, David Howell, who at times showed signs of political stage fright. But at no point did the GLC look likely to convince the Government to back down and legalise Fares Fair. It won the support of many Tory commu-ters who had enjoyed paying less for their season tickets, but it did not reach out and mobilise the anger of the people who were probably worst affected by the Law Lords' judgment – the poor, the unemployed and the house-bound women, for whom cheap fares had been a passport to greater freedom.

The continued defiance of the left did not last long. On February 8 the group passed a budget plan for the new financial year which implied acceptance of the fare increases and other manifesto defeats. And at council meetings on February 15 and 16, Labour members unanimously voted it through.

Over the next two months McDonnell, who had been the most effective of Livingstone's critics on the left, began to emerge as one of his closer political allies. In May, with Livingstone's backing, he was promoted by the group to the key chair of finance, where he gained a reputation for tough scrutiny of his colleagues' expenditure bids, pleased to expand spending, but determined to avoid wasteful over-budgeting. At the same elections Valerie Wise was appointed to chair a new women's committee, a pioneering venture since copied elsewhere, which produced an important base and resource centre for the women's movement. Dave Wetzel stayed in the transport chair and began to get down to the work of producing the 'balanced plan' of more modest fare reductions which the GLC eventually got through the courts in January 1983. Mike Ward stayed at industry to push through the painstaking detail of the job-creation strategy which he had prepared for the Labour manifesto. John Carr, as chairman of the staff committee, proceeded to implement the reforms of the equal opportunities policy. Tony McBrearty, who had supported McIntosh in preference to Livingstone in 1981, took over from Gladys Dimson as chair of housing and started to redefine the GLC's strategic housing role within the constraints of the earlier defeats. Sir Ashley Bramall, the former Labour leader of ILEA, whom Livingstone had once criticised so bitterly, was chosen by the group to be the next GLC chairman. So started what may be called the second Livingstone administration. The Labour group got down to the art of the possible.

The change was not lost on critics from the left. *London Labour Briefing*, which was then coming under the control of the Socialist Organiser faction of the Labour left, had attacked Livingstone's refusal to support Can't Pay Won't Pay. In its April issue there were four articles of fierce criticism against the 'compromising' policies of the GLC Labour group.

Keith Veness, a Chartist member of Islington Central CLP and one of Livingstone's long-standing political friends, wrote: 'As a result of the Denning and House of Lords judgments, the GLC is now being forced to tear up the main plank of our manifesto . . . a slow, gnawing process of disillusion is being started that will result in a gradual wasting of our support.'

He added: 'There is not now sufficient reason to stay in office [at the GLC], despite the plans in employment, education and housing. These are little more than palliatives and will neither generate the enthusiasm we need nor make up for the failure to confront our enemies in the Government and the Law Courts. Majority opposition is now the only honourable course for the comrades at County Hall to follow. A decision to do anything else is the road to disaster. This is the acid test to distinguish socialists from socialist administrators. It cannot and must not be ducked.'

In an open letter, John Bloxam and John O'Mahoney of Socialist Organiser said: 'You talk about doing better next time, in a different fight later. But if the GLC left will not fight for its main manifesto plank, what will it fight for?'

This is exactly the sort of argument which Livingstone himself would have deployed against previous generations of Labour leaders. Had he sold out?

Certainly Livingstone's political alibi was better than Goodwin's in 1975. He kept the faith until he was defeated by the council. But both Livingstone and Goodwin were overcome by surprise circumstances which were never envisaged in their manifestos. For Livingstone it was the Law Lords. For Goodwin it was hyperinflation, raging at 26 per cent. Both chose in the end to buckle down, stay in power and make the best of it.

Few people would blame Livingstone for this if he had not so bitterly blamed Goodwin at the GLC and Harold Wilson at national level. Livingstone's former adversaries will savour the language with which he now defends his position. 'Being defeated is not a betrayal,' he says. 'Carrying on fighting and using the building to carry on that fight is what the Labour movement expects its representatives to do. What they can't ever forgive is when they give up without a fight.'

Was this to suggest that, say, the Callaghan government had simply given up in the IMF crisis of 1976? 'At the time of the IMF there was an alternative strategy. It came from people with a radical approach – people like Crosland – who were prepared to say sod off to the IMF. We never had that sort of choice . . . And there's another difference. I think the Labour movement will forgive a Labour government that's blown off course and defeated provided it carries on and does all the other things which the IMF don't care a toss about. Even if the Labour Cabinet had given in and gone along with the IMF cuts, there was no justification not to do a whole range of other things like a Freedom of Information Act and bringing full gay rights to Northern Ireland. There's an endless range of things that a Labour government can do which proves that it is basically a decent radical government.'

So does Livingstone resent criticism from the left that he became a trimmer? 'I think it actually helps knowing that they are watching. Sometimes they are going to be unduly critical. But given the record of the last eighty years, who can blame them? Fine, you can go through a period when you get a lot of slagging off from the left. But if you carry on and you start to deliver, then over a period of months or years, people do actually respond.'

The GLC did indeed go on to deliver a great deal within the narrow areas left to it by the law. For now it may be worthwhile drawing together the strands of the story so far. Livingstone's failure to button up in the face of the early media campaign against him made him into a nationally-known politician, but also caused a serious strain on the loyalty of his Labour group. Heseltine's efforts to curb council spending changed the arithmetic of implementing the manifesto to such an extent that it began to seem politically impossible to achieve. The Labour group was plausibly heading for internal dislocation which Livingstone was in no position to control.

Then, due to a maverick legal challenge by the Bromley councillors, the cheap fares policy was outlawed. Efforts to defy the judgment and campaign against it gave Livingstone the best possible issue to win support for his policies and rehabilitate his popular image. The judgment also scaled down the cost of Labour's programme to manageable proportions. It moderated the left-wing councillors' aspirations and eventually created a surprising unity in the Labour group. Yet Livingstone continued to be attacked by the media for being a raving lefty, largely due to minor items of expenditure on grants to gays, feminists and blacks. People just failed to notice that on or about January 12, 1982, Livingstone's GLC went legit.

8 · Brent Crossed

Three weeks after the Law Lords' judgment, when the GLC Labour group's morale was at its lowest ebb, a giant sign was erected on top of County Hall showing the number of unemployed in London – an appalling total of 326,238. It was placed on a parapet, at an angle which made it clearly visible from the Houses of Parliament across the river, to provide a constant reminder of Labour outrage at the economic policies of the Thatcher administration.

This sign, which was updated each month to reflect the latest official jobless total, was the most public manifestation of the GLC's campaigning role in the wider forum of national politics. The ruling Labour group has used the council's resources of cash, expertise and public visibility to mount a running guerilla war against the Government. It has exhausted countless hours of civil servants' and Ministers' time by rooting out anomalies and eccentricities in legislation or statutory instruments and exploiting them for propaganda purposes.

For example, the GLC public services and fire brigade committee, an apparently humdrum appendage of municipal activity, tied the Home Office up in knots over regulations governing local authorities' responsibilities to plan for civil defence in case of nuclear war. Legal opinions were commissioned which enabled the committee chairman, Simon Turney, to prove that the GLC could evade Government orders to make civil defence preparations. This provided ammunition for about 150 other local authorities, which were declaring themselves nuclear free zones as a gesture of protest at Government defence and nuclear energy policies. It forced the Home Secretary to bring new regulations before Parliament in an attempt to enforce compliance with the Government's will.

These propaganda raids into the national political arena were

A message for the Government: Valerie Wise, Livingstone, Charlie Rossi, John McDonnell, Michael Ward, January 1982 (*Guardian*)

backed up in many cases by expensive advertising campaigns. Although GLC spending on them made little difference to the total rate bill – over the first three years of the Livingstone administration they cost Londoners only about 17p each – they were huge in comparison with conventional political practice. The result was that the council took on the appearance of a vigorous fighting machine in spite of its enforced inability to implement much of the expansion in services which Labour members had wanted to introduce. For Livingstone and the left, the use of the GLC as a platform for political expression gave ample compensation for defeats at the hands of Government and the law. Their unemployment sign could not actually reduce unemployment, but it could demonstrate a capacity to keep up the fight.

It might have been thought that this activity would have been welcomed by Labour's parliamentary team, which was trying to make unemployment and Britain's espousal of Cruise and Trident nuclear weapons systems the main thrust of its attack on the Thatcher government. In truth it was more of an irritant. Livingstone made no secret of the fact that he regarded the GLC as an 'alternative Opposition' which was doing the job because the Parliamentary Labour Party had feeble leadership and an excessive quota of right-wingers. Individual Labour MPs, including many on the left, also found it personally infuriating that Livingstone could summon a press conference and get his points across in the media, when their own speeches in the Commons went ignored by the political correspondents. MPs who had been vainly trying for years to get their views reported on issues (as opposed to the latest state of play in the Parliamentary personality battle) did not have their egos boosted by Livingstone's ability to discuss policies ad nauseum on the television screens.

A more serious problem for the Labour leader, Michael Foot, was that Livingstone was using the GLC platform not only to attack Margaret Thatcher, but also to launch a muscular assault on Foot himself. For example an editorial on November 20, 1981, in Livingstone's paper, *Labour Herald*, reprimanded Foot for criticising Tony Benn's decision to break ranks with the Parliamentary leadership in a Commons debate on energy policy. 'The message from the Party to its Parliamentary representatives must be ignore Foot and back Benn,' it said. *Labour Herald* kept up a running attack on the party's internal 'truce' agreement at Bishop's Stortford on the grounds that it muzzled the left while leaving the right free to 'witch-hunt' their opponents. The paper continued to argue against the expulsion of the Militant Tendency 'or the outlawing of any other Trotskyist group from the Labour Party' (26.3.82). It launched a virulent attack on Foot's stance over the 1982 Falklands war after he had supported the Government decision to send a naval task force: 'The only credible claim to sovereignty of the Malvinas is that of Argentina. It is the Argentine nation to which the claim attaches, not the corrupt junta which is currently in control of it' (7.5.82). In an editorial on the same day, headlined THREE YEARS OF NOT FIGHTING THATCHER, the paper condemned the party leadership's failure to provide a credible alternative in the face of the Government's 'concerted attack on British workers, particularly blacks, trade unionists and women.' It concluded:

There is a tendency on the Labour Left to assume that we have the policies to bring socialism, and all that is necessary is to remove those right-wingers in the PLP who do not support them. The fact is that our policies are not yet the policies of socialism. They are not yet developed to the stage where they point to a clear plan of campaign to defeat Thatcher and build socialism. They are not yet developed to the stage where they strike a chord in the consciousness of all those oppressed by this government. The clarification of our policies and the defeat of the Right in our Party go hand in hand. They must be our twin objectives in the battle for a clear, firm and united Labour Party. The next three years must not be wasted.

This general line of argument was backed up by comment on specific policies such as the NEC decision not to proceed with a pledge to nationalise the big four clearing banks. 'It is one more indication that the present leadership of the Labour Party is determined to make sure that the next Labour Government repeats the mistakes of the past.' The NEC plan for a 'people's Bank' was 'just about as appealing as yesterday's sweaty socks, and just about as likely to be adopted enthiastically by the voters' (6.8.82).

Such statements of opinion, repeated by Livingstone at political rallies around the country, were not exactly designed to endear him to the Labour leadership. Foot, a rebel himself for most of his political career, was not a man to be over-sensitive about attacks in a political weekly with a circulation of only about five thousand. He was bound to recognise, however, that derogatory statements by the Labour leader of the GLC fuelled discord within the party in a damagingly newsworthy way. Livingstone, along with other left-wingers like Peter Tatchell and Tariq Ali, became associated in Foot's mind with internal party trouble.

Foot was also unable to ignore Livingstone's repeated exposure in the mass circulation dailies over the issue of Northern Ireland. In spite of the criticism Livingstone received from within his Labour group for his remarks about the IRA in the wake of the 1981 Chelsea nail-bombing attack, he continued to use the platform of the GLC to plug away at the Irish issue, showing a degree of identification with the Sinn Fein cause which bordered on outright political support.

Although Sinn Fein was a political party which fought elections in Northern Ireland, its leaders backed the violent tactics of the Provisional IRA. This made it unacceptable, not only to the British government, but also to a wide range of Republican sentiment. For example on November 1, 1982, the then Irish Prime Minister Charles Haughey said 'that speaking on behalf of the overwhelming majority of the Irish people, North and South, I should immediately and categorically condemn the decision of the Sinn Fein Ard Fheis at the weekend to require their election candidates to be, in their words, "unambivalent in support of the armed struggle". This represents a serious and ominous development in our national life. No political organisation can adopt such a policy and be regarded as legitimate or democratic.'

Livingstone's involvement with Sinn Fein became a major issue of national attention in December 1982, following an invitation for two Sinn Fein leaders to visit London for private talks at County Hall. Inexplicably, as many as twenty-six members of the Labour group, including some previously stern critics of GLC involvement in Irish politics, had signed a letter circulated by Steve Bundred, vice-chairman of the GLC police committee, inviting Gerry Adams and Danny Morrison, newly-elected Sinn Fein members of the Northern Ireland Assembly, to come to London on December 14. The Labour group's political press officer was deliberately kept in the dark about the plan for fear that she would blow her top – the initiative was clearly going to upset her efforts to rehabilitate the GLC image in the eyes of Fleet Street and the electorate.

Bundred circulated his own press release, causing an initial flurry of hostile coverage in the national press on Monday December 6. That evening Michael Foot let it be known that he had sent a letter to Livingstone. It repudiated the Sinn Fein visit, but fell short of demanding that the invitation be withdrawn. He suggested Livingstone and his colleagues should tell their guests that the Labour Party was absolutely opposed to 'the barbarous methods of the Provos and other terrorist groups'.

Later that night, in one of the worst-ever atrocities in Northern Ireland, a bomb exploded at the Droppin Well pub disco in Ballykelly, County Derry, killing sixteen and injuring sixty-six. A device containing ten pounds of explosive had blown out the wall of the single-storey hall where about 150 people, half of them British soldiers, were drinking and dancing. This brought the reinforced concrete roof weighing many tons crashing down on to the crowded dance floor.

In the Commons the following day, the Prime Minister said it would be intolerable if the GLC invitation was not withdrawn. The SDP leader, Roy Jenkins, told Foot: 'Following the carnage at Ballykelly, it would be an outrage if the visit went ahead.'

But Livingstone did not back down. He put his name to a statement confirming the visit and suggested that the bombing was an attempt by the INLA to discredit the IRA's political wing. In its 'report' on Wednesday December 8, the *Sun* began: 'GLC leader Red Ken Livingstone became the most hated man in Britain last night after he insisted: The IRA's spokesmen are still welcome in London.'

Throughout that Tuesday and Wednesday the politicians' corridors at County Hall were besieged by journalists, putting tremendous pressure on the twenty-six signatories to the invitation to change their minds. Several who were disturbed at the turn events had taken were reluctant to be 'bullied' into cancelling the visit by what they regarded as media harassment. Others became convinced that, however right it might have been to invite Sinn Fein, it was impossible to have a rational discussion with them in the charged political atmosphere after Ballykelly.

During Wednesday, Foot had a private discussion with Living-

stone at which he urged him to withdraw the invitation. Livingstone said he would report the leader's views to a meeting the
following afternoon of the twenty-six signatories. That meeting,
which plausibly would have forced Livingstone into an embarrassing retreat, never took place. On the Wednesday evening, the
Home Secretary signed exclusion orders under the Prevention of
Terrorism Act banning Adams and Morrison from entering
mainland Britain. The Act entitled the Home Secretary to exclude
anyone who 'is or has been . . . involved in the commission,
preparation or instigation of acts of terrorism'. So, once again,
Livingstone was allowed to escape from a difficult political corner
by having the decision taken out of his hands. Sinn Fein was able
to argue that the Home Secretary's decision 'proves what we have
been saying all along, that the British Government fears the
message which Republicans wish to deliver, and were prepared at
their peril to deliver, to concerned politicians in London. We want
to see an end to the war in our country and we believe that peace
can only be achieved when the British withdraw, allow the Irish
people the right to self-determination and allow the Irish people to
resolve their differences. It is now ludicrous for the British
Government to claim that the Six Counties are part of the United
Kingdom and then go and exclude its so-called citizens from
entering one part of Britain – London.'

This propaganda victory for Sinn Fein was consolidated by
Livingstone in an article in the *Times* on December 11. 'The
exclusion order is a peculiar device,' he wrote. 'If there is any
evidence that the Sinn Fein representatives are involved in terrorism, then they should be arrested and charged. On the other hand,
if they are free to walk the streets of Belfast, then they should be
free to do so in London. The real explanation of the ban is that it is
a response to the hysteria whipped up by the press.' Livingstone
stated that he deplored all acts of violence without qualification
and concluded: 'The lesson to be drawn from the history of
Ireland is that force cannot be used to impose a solution. Therefore at some point a dialogue must begin. Those who have condemned our initiative must say what they propose as an alternative. Or are they prepared to see another thirteen years of horror?'

Press Officer Nita Clarke, Livingstone and Gerry Adams of Sinn Fein, July 1983 (*Güardian*)

At a GLC council meeting on December 14 (the day the Sinn Fein talks would have been held), Livingstone was defeated in a censure motion moved by the Conservatives over the issue of the invitation. Nine of his fellow Labour councillors abstained. This was one of three occasions in Livingstone's political career when members of his own party have allowed opposition censure motions to succeed. Each time he carried on regardless.

The affair totally obscured the Labour group's attempt to win support for a new round of London Transport fare cuts which it was preparing to take through the courts. It also masked efforts to embarrass the Tories by setting up an inquiry into councillors' links with housing associations. But, in spite of criticism from other GLC Labour councillors, Livingstone continued to push the Irish issue. On February 26, 1983, he went to Northern Ireland for a weekend visit as the guest of Sinn Fein. Before he flew back the next day he told a press conference that Provisional

Sinn Fein 'is not the caricature that it is made out to be'. It was, he said, developing socialist policies and a desire for peace. On July 26, 1983, Gerry Adams visited London at the invitation of Livingstone and Jeremy Corbyn (by then Labour MP for Islington North). Adams had won the Parliamentary election in Belfast West, but refused to take his seat. He said he saw the visit as part of a long-term attempt to open up a dialogue with the British people and their representatives and to break down the 'wall of disinformation' erected by the British government around Northern Ireland. The visit allowed Adams unprecedented opportunity to put his views over to the public in extended television interviews.

On August 26, 1983, Livingstone said on Irish state radio that what Britain had done to Ireland over eight hundred years was worse than what Hitler had done to the Jews in the Second World War. His views were condemned by contenders for the Labour leadership: 'extraordinarily eccentric,' said Neil Kinnock; 'absurd and offensive,' said Roy Hattersley; 'inflicting shame on the whole Labour Party,' said Peter Shore; and 'most unfortunate Ken Livingstone put it the way that he did,' said Eric Heffer.

On each of these occasions, Livingstone's association with Sinn Fein fuelled major controversy in the media. His stance also contributed to a breakdown of relations between the GLC and London's monopoly evening newspaper, the *Standard*. The GLC withdrew all its advertising from the *Standard* to try to force it to print an apology for a cartoon by Jak which Livingstone held to be offensively anti-Irish. The Press Council subsequently condemned the GLC's action as 'a blatant attempt by a local authority to use the power of its purse to influence the contents of a newspaper and coerce the editor.' Livingstone called the Press Council 'an appalling Tory body' and kept up the advertising ban. By doing so, he ensured continuing hostility from a paper which might otherwise have been more inclined to support the GLC in its later fights with the Government. Livingstone cannot deny that he allowed his commitment to British withdrawal from Northern Ireland to get in the way of his domestic responsibilities as leader of the GLC. Nor does he wish to do so. (The explanation of his stance on Ireland, which follows, dates from an interview before

The controversial Jak cartoon, *Standard*, October 29, 1982 (*Jak*)

the 'worse than Hitler' episode and his subsequent apology for any offence this might have caused to the Jewish community.)

'Don't underestimate how important it is to me that we eventually get Britain out of Ireland.' Why? 'If you read anything of Irish history, you read it with a sense of outrage ... It's a most appalling record. It ranks with the way some of the Middle Eastern races have been liquidated by the Turkish Empire or the Russians. It rates worse than the way in which the Kurds have been butchered by virtually everyone around them from time to time. It is the most appalling chapter. It spans 800 years, but it's as bad in those 800 years as what Hitler did to the Jews in six. It's only because it's spread over 800 years that we don't see it in such horrifying terms.

'Before the potato famine, the population of Ireland was eight million and I think at that time Britain's was fifteen million or more – something of that order.

'The population of Ireland today is still only five million. Ireland has never recovered. It is the only country most probably anywhere in the world where the population today is less than it was in Napoleonic times . . . We actually forced everyone to leave. Look at the history. Whilst we controlled it, we didn't allow them to develop industry. We actually kept it as a sort of client state in which the peasants were forced to buy our goods, not allowed to develop their own industry, not allowed to hold their own land.

'If you read any of the detailed histories of Ireland you boil with outrage. It is worse than all the Boers have done to the blacks in South Africa, which chills the blood of *Guardian* readers . . . We can see and tackle our own racism about black people and the classic *Guardian* liberal does that beautifully. Even if they feel a nasty anti-black thought bubbling up, they are going to stamp on it. But the racism against the Irish is so much deeper. It isn't expressed by many people crudely in the anti-Irish jokes, but it's expressed in a way that people don't perceive as racism. You hear people say things like: we have to be there to prevent them killing themselves. There is the absolute moral arrogance that somehow we are more able to control that situation than the Irish themselves, ignoring our major role in the butchery over the years . . .

When Livingstone talks like this about Ireland, unscripted, unprepared, he is charged with a political electricity which is only otherwise seen when he is under heavy attack in the council chamber or at the emotional peak of a major platform speech. Where does it come from? Not, surely, from a Scots father and a south London mother?

'It's just been a slow growth. The more I've read, the more I am outraged. I'm more outraged today than I was twelve months ago, because I've read more.' But was this reason enough to put his GLC administration at risk and court the wrath of the Parliamentary leadership? 'Hang on. I believe we've actually won the debate on Ireland. Compare where we are now with where we were two years ago . . . Two years ago the Irish in London were frightened to discuss the question of British withdrawal. If you were in a pub and someone came round collecting for Sinn Fein, you'd think twice about putting money in the box because you might be done

"Dear Mr Livingstone. With the price of nails being what it is, we wondered whether the GLC . . ." *Daily Mail*, October 14, 1981

for supporting an illegal organisation. The Special Branch would just say it was for the IRA and you'd have no chance coming up in court arguing about that.

'Now people in the Irish community actually feel they can debate why Britain should get out. Two years of activity have allowed hundreds of thousands of men and women in this country to say honestly what they believe about the history of Ireland. It's moved the Labour Party very far over in its thinking. And I believe we will soon get to a position where the Labour Party ends up by being committed to removing the Unionist veto on withdrawal.

'We didn't plan how we would raise the issue . . . but by sticking firm and not giving in and doing what the media demanded I do each time – which was just to make a solitary condemnation of the IRA and ignore the troops that shoot the face of a child with a plastic bullet – by standing firm we have moved the entire area of the public debate through about 90 degrees.'

Most members of the Parliamentary Labour Party would regard this assessment as fanciful. Most have bitterly resented Livingstone's forays into a subject about which they think he knows little and understands nothing. But, if they could suspend their disbelief and ask Livingstone whether it was worth allowing the Irish issue to put the GLC Labour programme at risk, his answer would be this.

'It is conflicting. I'm asked to choose all the time. It undoubtedly would be easier to say we'll just concentrate on GLC issues. But that involves me ignoring what is happening in Ireland. I can't do that. I don't actually want to do that. I don't want to save local government by doing nothing for Ireland. I think it's an obscene calculation to make because people are dying over there . . .

'There wouldn't be one per cent of doubt in my mind about sacrificing the whole of British local government if it meant we got out of Ireland. The two principles cannot be equated: the organisation of local services within the state cannot be weighed against the right of the Irish to be free.'

It must be starting to become clear why Livingstone provokes such a deep sense of loathing among most of the Labour Party establishment. They regarded it as impertinent for a mere councillor to challenge party policy in this way over Ireland and other national issues. But the impertinence was compounded by Livingstone's continuing ability to divert media attention towards himself and away from the mainstream leadership. Above all, they believed that he was a major loser of votes for the Labour Party – that every time he opened his mouth he disaffected another few thousand of the white Anglo-Saxon heterosexual working class which formed the bedrock of the party's electoral strength. Livingstone's leading opponents in the Shadow Cabinet and NEC do not like gracing him with public statements of criticism. A distillation of their views would be that he and his colleagues at County Hall are a group of 'political pre-adolescents' who have turned London into an 'adventure playground' for a 'variety of zany left-wing causes' which have alienated 'ordinary' people; that they have preferred 'ineffectual sloganising' to getting on with the job of improving local services; and that Livingstone has bent his 'undoubted talents' to fighting internal party wars 'in complete forgetfulness of the impact on the wider electorate'.

When the Party conference in October 1982 produced a shift to the right on the NEC, Livingstone became exposed to determined efforts to block his political advancement. For John Golding, variously described as 'witch-hunter general' and 'organising genius of the right' on the NEC, the task of keeping Livingstone out of Parliament became one of the top priorities for rehabilitating Labour's image in the eyes of the electorate. The scene was set for the battle of Brent East.

Within weeks of gaining the leadership of the GLC, Livingstone was receiving overtures from activists in several London constituencies that they would like him to be their Labour candidate at the next general election. He says he rejected an exploratory invitation from Islington South and later a firm approach from Newham North-West because he felt an 'affinity' for the constituency of Brent East where friends and supporters were urging him to stand. Brent East is a predominantly working-class area, including a high proportion of ethnic Irish voters, in a part of north-west London around Kilburn, Neasden, Willesden and Cricklewood. Livingstone's efforts to win the Labour nomination there involved deselecting Reg Freeson, its sitting Labour MP since 1964. The selection battle between these two men became one of the bitterest and hardest-fought tests of constituency parties' new rights to reselect their candidates following the constitutional changes won by the left at the Labour Party conferences of 1979 and 1980. It ended in the opening days of the 1983 general election campaign when the Brent East party stopped just short of court action to challenge the Labour NEC's decision to veto a selection contest which Livingstone seemed certain to win. The result was that his ambition to become an MP was thwarted for another Parliamentary term. Barring apparently remote by-election chances, he could not enter the Commons until he was the wrong side of forty. The circumstances surrounding this set-back provide further evidence of Livingstone's style of operation and why the Labour Party establishment regarded him as a threat.

"Mr Livingstone, I presume?"

"Mr Livingstone, I presume!"

Two minds with but a single joke; *Daily Mail*, June 26, 1981 . . . and *Daily Telegraph*, March 1, 1983

To the outsider it seems inconceivable that anyone could have felt 'affinity' for the Labour parties in Brent East or Brent South which, in the early 1980s, were going through a period of internecine strife. The left challenged the right's hegemony on the local borough council and the right tried to fight back. On September 5, 1981, officials of the London Labour Party conducted an inquiry into allegations of malpractice at councillor selection meetings for the St Raphael's branch of Brent South. To judge by their report, considered by the NEC on September 23, it appears they never got to the bottom of counter-allegations by right and left of widespread political skulduggery. The NEC ruled that shortlisting and selection proceedings at St Raphael's should be declared void. A new selection meeting was held on February 22, 1982, attended by an assistant regional organiser. Her private report to head office provides moving testimony of the appalling state of Brent Labour Party politics into which Livingstone was about to move:

The usual chaos prevailed, with challenge and counter-challenge. I presided over this selection meeting to the best of my ability. I interpreted the rulings from the National Agent to the best of my ability and conforming to the standards of strict neutrality not only expected, but welcomed, by the full-time organising staff of the Labour Party. As a result I was verbally abused and battered to such an extent that I was still smarting the following day.

I don't say that this meeting met the standards that we would like to stand by, but I will say that the attendance register matched the list of agreed members submitted by St Raphael's branch and agreed as a basis of membership by the National Agent. I cannot say there was no collusion or buying of membership, but I can say that I would have difficulty proving that there was and I would not care to enter into that particular arena. The arguments in the CLPs [Constituency Labour Parties] in Brent will continue, if we are honest with ourselves, until such times as the LGC [Local Government Committee] is sorted out and I don't think there is much we can do about that. This may not be the right vehicle nor the time to say it, but why not. The morale of the organising staff is at a very low ebb and this kind of debate does not help . . .

On February 24, Brent South's Labour MP, Laurie Pavitt, wrote to the national agent, David Hughes, enclosing a photostat copy of a cheque, allegedly used to join up a block of members at the selection meeting. Hughes replied that he had tried to arrange a selection 'that bears some semblance to a fair process according to the Rules of the Party. So far this has proved almost impossible to achieve . . . It does seem to need something of a miracle now to sort it all out.'

On March 30, George Page, general secretary of the Greater London Labour Party, wrote to Hughes:

I am afraid the troubles continue in Brent. Despite all attempts to unite the Party, carried out by the four of us in this office, the disruptive influences continue to undermine our work and all we suffer is personal abuse and misrepresentation. I fear very much for the Borough elections there, and if steps are not soon taken to stop the internal wars permanent damage to the Labour Party in the whole Borough is likely.

Because of the continuing dispute between St Raphael's and Brent South, and the actions of the Local Government Committee, I urge the NEC to conduct an inquiry. There are many other parts of Brent where peace only appears to reign because many good comrades have grown sick of the behaviour of others, and have given up.

On April 30 Hughes reported to the NEC: 'The Local Government Committee for the London Borough of Brent and the Brent South Constituency Party have caused problems for twelve months now concerning the selection of a candidate for the St Raphael's Ward. A selection has now been made which must stand but the atmosphere created in the Branch and Party leaves much to be desired.' The NEC backed his recommendation that a committee of inquiry be set up 'into the management of the Party Organisation in the London Borough of Brent'. On May 10 its organisation committee appointed Eric Heffer, Neil Kinnock and David Hughes to do the job.

The purpose of this swift detour through the party's Brent files is not to make judgments of blame against left or right which party officials themselves felt unable to offer. It is to show the degree of antagonism which existed in the local parties and to explain why the Brent East party failed to go through the procedure for reselecting its Parliamentary candidate at the proper time. The rules say that reselection should take place between eighteen months and three years after a general election, but in Brent reselection was postponed until after the local elections and the various internal party inquiries were out of the way. This time-lapse became crucial to Livingstone's eventual defeat by the centre and right-wing majority on the NEC.

But why was it that he chose to make his Parliamentary bid in what appears to have been one of the most unpleasantly acrimonious constituencies in the country? Livingstone explains that there were a number of people living in Brent East whom he had known politically for years – friends on the hard left, like Paul Franklin and Frank Hansen, and others with whom he had worked at various times, like Mike Grabina, Martin Coleman and John Mordecai (his personal assistant in his days as Camden housing chairman). 'On top of that, from when I arrived in Hampstead as Parliamentary candidate in June 1976, I had been getting a lot of publicity in the local papers which covered both areas. When I then became Paddington GLC member, the papers covered that area as well . . . So the party activists knew me quite well.'

Believe him if you wish, Livingstone adds: 'I'd always been in the position of being happy to stand in Brent and yet not sufficiently eager to get into Parliament to go stomping around looking for a seat – the way some other people have done – I like the actual area. There is a very warm response from people in Brent, not party activists, but ordinary voters. I'd been up and down the Kilburn High Road for years. I eat in the Indian restaurants there. You just get a friendly reaction. It's an area I would like to represent. There's an affinity I think.'

Relations between officers of the Brent East constituency party and its MP, Reg Freeson, became increasingly strained during 1981. In letters to the party secretary, Ron Anderson, on March 10, July 7 and August 10, Freeson complained about the local party's failure to invite him to speak at its public meetings. He subsequently argued that he was given few opportunities to make the MP's customary Parliamentary reports to GMC meetings; that he was denied access to party members' names and addresses so that he was unable to send them Parliamentary reports or other political messages; and that it was made impossible for him to meet new party members.

Freeson, who had been brought up in the West Norwood Jewish Orphanage, was by no means a right-winger. He was a founder-member of CND, a consistent opponent of Britain's membership of the EEC and a supporter of the re-unification of Ireland. So although he was getting on increasingly prickly terms with the officers of the Brent East party, it was quite possible that he could have won support for his reselection from the independent left-wingers in the local party who far outnumbered activists associated with particular hard-left tendencies.

Livingstone says that both the old-guard council leadership on the right and the Chartist and Socialist Organiser factions on the hard left pursued 'very over-the-top tactics' during the rows over selection of council candidates. He blames the old council leader, John Lebor, for starting the aggravation, but he acknowledges that the hard left's behaviour alienated a substantial body of opinion on the softer left. Livingstone was being pushed by the Chartists for Brent East Parliamentary nomination, although he was strongly opposed by Socialist Organiser. So Freeson had a chance of isolating him and winning a reselection majority with the support of the main body of independent left-wingers.

Freeson failed to make the most of this opportunity. Several of the leading members of the independent left in the constituency approached him during the summer of 1982 and urged him to lead a fight back against the hard left. Freeson made it clear to them that he did not have the stomach for it. If he could be reselected as candidate, all well and good, but he did not want to become involved in factional in-fighting. Freeson gave the soft left the impression that for both personal and political reasons he was ready to turn his back on the whole sorry business.

According to Livingstone's account: 'After their last meeting with Freeson, the soft left people invited me to go and see them . . . I made it quite clear that I was not prepared to join them in a purge of the hard left, but equally I was not prepared to join the hard left in a purge of them.

'The two groups had got to work together. We didn't come to

any conclusion. We were just all quite frank for an evening. Then people went away on their holidays. By the time they came back in September, the soft left, without taking any formal decision about it, had basically come to the conclusion that most of them would vote for me. And that gave me the majority . . .

'I think I was ideally placed as candidate to work with both those groups and weld them together. And it started to work, because as soon as the soft left decided to support me, the hard left started being much more pleasant to them.'

In wooing the centre (that is the Brent East centre – from the perspective of Westminster and the Labour Party HQ all Livingstone's supporters were deemed pretty extreme), Livingstone did not extricate himself from the battle on the hard left. On August 29 a letter was circulated by Pete Firmin, a constituency branch secretary, to more than sixty members on the left of the Brent East party. This letter formed the basis of Freeson's subsequent allegation that he was being opposed by a form of caucus activity which is outlawed under the Labour Party constitution. It said:

Dear Comrade, I have been asked to convene a meeting of Brent East Labour Left on September 12th to decide on a left candidate for the parliamentary selection procedure. This follows a preliminary meeting held on Sunday July 4th attended by 16 people (from 7 Brent East Branches) at which it was agreed to invite 'prospective' candidates whose names were put forward to a further meeting (it was also agreed that this should be on September 12). After discussion, particularly about whether a local person should be encouraged to stand, the only names put forward were those of Ken Livingstone (GLC Leader) and Gerry Byrne (of Putney CLP). Both of these have been invited and have agreed to attend on September 12th.

At the first meeting it was agreed that it is essential that we have a united left candidate if we are to stand a chance of defeating R. Freeson, and it was thus agreed by all present that they would back (i.e. seek nomination for, argue for, and, where applicable, vote for) whoever wins a majority at the 12th September meeting, as this is the only way for the Left to make the necessary impact on the selection. This second meeting is thus open to all members of the Brent East CLP who accept the need for a Left replacement of Freeson as prospective parliamentary candidate, and agree to back the united Left candidate . . .

The meeting took place at the Trades and Labour Hall in Willesden. According to Livingstone, it was a ploy by Socialist Organiser to win support for its candidate, Ms Gerry Byrne. 'The whole of the meeting was a debate about whether or not there should be a woman candidate. No one discussed the word mandating. It wasn't even used. The whole debate was about whether or not I should be a woman. It was quite a good-humoured debate about the inadequacy of my not being a woman.'

Inadequate or not, a vote was taken in which Livingstone beat Byrne by 37 votes to 16. On September 17 the story was carried in the local paper, the *Brent Chronicle*, under the headline RED KEN V REG: SECRET BID TO DUMP BRENT MP. It predicted renewed civil war in the Brent East party in selection procedures which it expected to begin in October.

That reselection process, however, never happened. In an unrelated development on September 22, Labour's NEC approved the recommendation of the committee of inquiry under Eric Heffer, Neil Kinnock and David Hughes, set up more than four months before to investigate alleged malpractices in the selection of some candidates for the council elections. They reported that it was 'impossible to test the truth of the allegations made'. And they concluded: 'We believe that in the interests of fair play all round and that of the officers in particular there is a need for close supervision of the running of the Brent Local Government Committee and the Brent South and East Constituency Labour Parties for at least six months.' Joyce Gould, the assistant national agent and chief women's officer, was given this unenviable supervisory job. The reselection process was put on ice pending her report. So although it was widely assumed in the press that Livingstone had the nomination sewn up, Freeson and opponents of Livingstone on the NEC began to realise that they had the chance to freeze him out.

Freeson, who had been almost ready to chuck in his hand during the summer, was outraged by the left caucus meeting of September 12. As he sat in the Labour Party conference in Blackpool later that month, without yet knowing how to topple Livingstone, he became determined to make a fight of it.

On October 27 he wrote to the party's general secretary, Jim Mortimer, listing thirty-eight complaints about what had gone on in Brent East. He said that, until these matters had been investigated, 'effective supervision will not be possible'. Freeson argued that the Brent East Labour left preselection meeting on September 12 seriously prejudiced his position. And he concluded: 'I think that the information available shows clearly that there has been serious unconstitutional conduct over the Parliamentary candidature and that anything arising from it should be considered invalid.' In Freeson's eyes the September 12 meeting had been a caucus which mandated those present to vote for Livingstone at any official selection meeting which might follow. According to Livingstone, there could be no question of mandating because the final selection would have been by secret ballot. His argument was that he merely attended a meeting, organised by political opponents from Socialist Organiser, which was no more sinister (and much less disciplined) than meetings run by trades unions in many constituencies to choose a candidate to back at selection meetings.

Rubbish, argued Freeson. Livingstone had not just turned up to an event run by opponents. He had been closely involved in planning the meeting, which was run formally as if it were a selection procedure, with candidates, speeches and manifestos. People, some of whom did not even live in the constituency, had been invited to it by name.

This row was never settled. On October 25, the national agent, David Hughes, wrote to Pete Firmin (the man who signed the invitation letter) expressing concern about the phrases 'agree to back the United Left candidate' and 'discuss various aspects of the fight to replace Freeson', which he thought suggested there might be an attempt to mandate delegates. But the NEC decided to defer investigation of Freeson's complaint until after Gould's six-month inquiry was completed.

On March 7, 1983, Freeson wrote again to Jim Mortimer. This time he pointed out that clause 14(7) of the party constitution stipulated that, in the case of a sitting Labour MP, the reselection process *must* start within three years of the last general election.

Since three years and ten months had elapsed, he asked for guidance from the NEC. Freeson's argument was that the Brent East general management committee had failed to carry out a reselection in time and that it was by then too late to start one.

At its meeting on March 23, the NEC decided to seek legal advice on the matter from Lord Milner of Leeds. The Brent East party responded by asking for a counsel's opinion from Lord Gifford. Gifford struck first, advising the Brent party on April 4 that they had a legal responsibility to begin a reselection as soon as possible. Milner responded with a view that the NEC was entitled to take the matter into its own hands and dispense with the normal reselection procedure.

Meanwhile Joyce Gould had completed her six-month period of supervision of the Brent parties. In her report to the NEC she noted the facts of the preselection meeting of the Brent East Labour left without passing judgment on them. She concluded that the Brent parties 'were now operating with the rules and constitution of the party'. This removed one obstacle to reselection going ahead. On April 20 and 24 the Brent East party secretary wrote to Jim Mortimer requesting the NEC's cooperation in agreeing a reselection timetable. On April 27 the NEC decided not to allow reselection to proceed. The next day the Brent East GMC agreed by seventy-one votes to four to go ahead anyway on the basis of the Gifford legal opinion. The affair seemed to be heading inexorably towards a battle in the courts between the constituency party and the NEC.

On May 9, however, Margaret Thatcher went to the Palace to request the dissolution of Parliament for the general election. David Hughes, the national agent, wrote to the Brent East secretary citing a special rule which ensured the automatic re-selection of sitting MPs if the normal selection procedures had not been completed before Parliament was dissolved: 'Therefore Mr Reg Freeson is the Labour Party candidate for the Brent East constituency in the General Election to be held on 9 June 1983.'

On May 11, the NEC decided by a majority of nineteen votes to nine to endorse this interpretation. Only Tony Benn, Frank Allaun, Judith Hart, Eric Heffer, Jo Richardson, Audrey Wise, Dennis

Skinner, Tom Sawyer and Lawrence Coates voted for reselection to go ahead.

For a few days the Brent East party refused to back down. It threatened court action and went ahead with arrangements for a selection conference on May 18. When the day arrived, however, the local party reluctantly accepted the NEC decision. According to a letter sent by its secretary to the national agent: 'A vote was then taken by a show of hands as to who we would have liked to have selected had we been allowed. This resulted in 53 votes for Ken Livingstone and 2 votes for Reg Freeson, with 3 abstentions.'

On June 9, Freeson won his seventh Parliamentary election in the constituency. His majority was cut to 4,834, but, allowing for small boundary changes, the notional swing from Labour to the Conservatives was less than 1 per cent, compared with an inner London average of 2.3 per cent and an outer London average of 4.6 per cent. In spite of – or was it because of – all the fuss, Labour in Brent East did comparatively well.

This Brent saga is a sad episode in Labour history from which nobody emerged with much credit. At no stage did the NEC decide the rights and wrongs of the affair, preferring instead to play for time until the election was called.

Livingstone's view is that he lost out purely because the NEC elections in 1982 produced a right-wing executive under the sway of John Golding. 'What the Golding majority on the NEC were trying to do was to ensure that in the aftermath of the election there was the minimum hard-left presence in the Parliamentary Labour Party so that Kinnock or Hattersley would be able to emerge as the eventual choice of the party in the succession [to Foot]. I think they were thinking that far ahead.'

In truth opposition to Livingstone was probably more personal. Rightly or wrongly he was perceived by much of the NEC as Labour's biggest potential loser of votes in the country. He had to be kept out as a sign that Labour was not the party of the so-called loony left. Livingstone's problem was that he was too well known. He became the victim of his own image-building.

9 · Trotsky and the Apes

Well, is he a Trot or isn't he? In the demonology of the Labour Party establishment there is an archetypal figure, variously called 'bedsitter revolutionary', 'paperback Marxist' or member of the 'lumpen polytechnic', who emerged from a sociology department at some point in the late 1960s to begin a life of political disruption, during which he – or just as probably she – 'infiltrated' the Labour Party and, by a mixture of unpleasantness and stamina for long boring meetings, drove away its 'salt-of-the-earth' working-class members, pushed through 'extremist' policy resolutions and condemned Labour to a generation of electoral unpopularity. It must be clear from the story so far that Livingstone is not such a person. When he joined Norwood Labour Party in 1968, it was already virtually empty and he was ideologically vague, a young man who was casting around for ideas to explain his disappointment at the Wilson government's failure to match up to the 'trembling of excitement' he had felt at its outset in 1964. With a talent for public speaking, and in the absence of any local competition, he almost immediately took his place on Lambeth borough council. There he was appalled at the record of the old-guard Labour politicians who, in the face of the borough's chronic housing stress, had lagged behind the rest of London in getting moving on a rebuilding and modernisation programme. Even the Tories in their brief spell in office had done better than old Alderman Cotton and his Labour crew. What was perhaps even worse, the whole idea of public-sector housing provision had become devalued by what Livingstone saw as the oppressive and distant bureaucracy of council officialdom.

Before he had a chance to work out his own ideas, he was immediately cast in an executive role as housing vice-chairman, responsible for these housing management problems; and he made some instinctive lunges towards liberalising the system until he was blocked and forced to resign his office. At this time Ted Knight, who had found him 'a centrist member of the Labour Party' in 1970, began to exert an influence on Livingstone's political development. By a process of argument on individual issues within the debates of the Norwood party, he gave Livingstone some of the 'perspective' which he himself had gained through a much more formal ideological training. So Livingstone aligned himself with the hard left inside the Labour Party and this alignment was consolidated by his experiences on the GLC in 1975 where he believed that the Goodwin administration had betrayed its manifesto.

At no stage, however, did Livingstone feel inclined to join any of the hard left factions. This was partly because he was throughout a practical and ambitious politician engaged in real-world decisions on councils; and partly because he had an early sense of the futility of the left's tendency to splinter into tiny, mutually antagonistic grouplets arguing how many revolutionaries could dance on the head of a pin. So Livingstone came to work with the hard left without ever really belonging to any part of it. He was for the left, but not typically of the left.

The alliances he formed, from Labour Against Housing Cuts in 1975 through to the Brent East selection battles of 1983, were umbrella groupings to fight specific campaigns. He was never too choosy about who joined him under the umbrella, preferring, as he puts it, 'to approach each issue empirically, asking how do you mobilise the largest amount of support to achieve a specific policy end at any point in time'.

Livingstone's relationship with individual left groups blew hot and cold through the 1970s, as alliances formed and re-formed around particular issues. 'What I've always avoided doing is actually joining anything,' he says, 'because then you are involved in accepting a whole range of policy positions which it is most probably impossible to do. You can't find any one grouping on the left that I would agree with.'

Chance played a big part in the actual alliances which were formed. Politics does not work along rules of economic theory where everyone behaves rationally because everyone knows what everyone else is doing. People tend to team up with the people they know. For example in 1978 when Livingstone joined the Socialist Campaign for Labour Victory, another more mainstream Bennite coalition was being formed in the Labour Co-ordinating Committee. Livingstone says he sent off his £5 to join the LCC and received one mailing from them, but heard nothing more for the next five years. 'Life is full of those sort of things. It's not planned. The people pulling together the LCC had no base in local government . . . Also I was largely unknown outside of London lefty circles. I'd never even spoken to Tony Benn until June 1979.'

Livingstone rejects the charge that in these alliances he has been politically careless by lining himself up with left-wing groups which were pursuing the classic Trotskyist 'transitional programme' (promoting unrealistic demands which a capitalist society cannot concede if it is to survive). 'You are characterising the left too generally,' he suggests. 'They do want to achieve power. Undoubtedly there are a small group of people running around in the Labour movement with a purely revolutionary perspective. When they come into the Labour Party it is either to destroy it, or to try to take it over, or to expose contradictions in it. But the overwhelming majority of people on what you would call the hard left have the objective of electing a Labour government and getting it to make . . . a series of changes by stages.

'There are some groups on the left, like the Spartacists who say that you've got to destroy the Labour Party and that people like me are more dangerous than the Tories because we give illusions to the workers that we can achieve change. There's a degree of that sort of thinking in Socialist Organiser and it can be seen more specifically in the Socialist Workers Party and Revolutionary Communist Party. Those are the small grouplets on the left who take the view that you have got to destroy the Labour Party before the workers can really surge forwards. So I have great difficulty working with them and they spend a lot of their time slagging me off. Then you've got this other range of views like Socialist Action and the old Chartists, groups like the Campaign for Labour Party Democracy and LCC, and there I've had a very good working relationship, although sometimes we fall out.'

So Livingstone explains his tactics as follows: 'You mobilise the maximum vote behind you at any one time to ensure that you win. You cannot work in politics on the basis that you put together an alliance and ten years later it's still there plodding away. Attitudes in alliances shift so rapidly. They do within the left groupings as much as they do within the national leadership of the party. People that hate, loathe and detest each other in the top four or five positions of the party for two or three years then are driven together by circumstances and work in a wonderful warm loving relationship for three or four years until they fall out again.' (Livingstone illustrates the point with reference to Wilson and Callaghan.)

It is time to repeat the question. Is he a Trot or isn't he? 'If you did one of those multiple-choice tests, where you are forced to choose: are you a Stalinist, or a Trot, or a Social Democrat? – you'd most probably end up being forced to put me down as a Trot by a process of elimination. But I think there's a real problem characterising politicians. You can characterise political groupings because they are made up of the sum total of the individuals in them and because they carry a set of intellectual baggage to which the individuals tend to adapt and conform. But when you are talking about an individual politician there is always such a strange mixture of views and things that have happened in their past that it's very difficult to make a simple characterisation. At the end of the day you can only say: well, if you've read the book, you know what Ken Livingstone is, but you can't shorten it down to a sentence.'

This answer illuminates the suspicion which political activists of many shades of opinion have about Livingstone. They cannot place him politically. Take the view of Roy Shaw, who as leader of Camden council on the old Tribunite wing of the Labour Party, bore the brunt of Livingstone's attacks from the left: 'He embraces Marxism if he thinks it will be of advantage to him. But he certainly is not a Marxist. He plays along with them and uses a lot of their methods, but he certainly is not one of them.'

Or Andrew McIntosh, whom Livingstone deposed for the leadership of the GLC: 'I am twelve years older than he is. He will end up to the right of me. I have, I think, an analytical approach to the issues of economic equality and political decentralisation. I don't think he has any general political views . . . He reminds me of the young Tories and right-wing Labour people who were at Oxford with me in the 1950s. They saw their progress as being in the centre – Butskellism was the key to advancement. Today the committee chairmen of the GLC see their way to advancement as being on the "radical" left. I don't think there is an ounce of radicalism in any of them. They don't really want to shake things up . . . So I don't think of [Livingstone] as an ideological antagonist in any way.'

Some of Livingstone's critics have suggested that it is this ideological imprecision which allows him to stray beyond the natural boundaries of the Labour Party to get to parts of the left which a true Labour man should not reach. There is bewilderment, for example, about his willingness to have contact with the Workers Revolutionary Party whose aims and perspectives are incompatible with Labour Party membership.

The WRP paper, the *News Line*, has broadly supported Livingstone's policy line at the GLC, even on occasions when Livingstone was adopting an apparently moderate position (such as his opposition to the Can't Pay Won't Pay campaign against the Law Lords' judgment). In return Livingstone has spoken twice on *News Line* or WRP platforms.

Livingstone says there is no difference between the support he has received from the *News Line* and the support the Labour Party leadership received from the *Morning Star* (at the time when it was the organ of the Communist Party of Great Britain). In neither case, he says, does such support imply political liaison. Nor does his appearance on a *News Line* platform suggest a relationship with the WRP, any more than his decision to speak at a Conservative Party conference rally in 1983 might suggest he is a Tory.

He acknowledges that the WRP's predecessor, the SLL, made a couple of efforts to recruit him around 1972 after he had helped to provide sleeping accommodation in council property for their unemployment protest marchers. He says he declined the invitation because he never wanted to join one particular left grouping and had no contact with the WRP from 1972 to 1981 when the *News Line* started to interview him about the GLC. 'It's the lack of that sectarian involvement that makes it possible to work with a whole range of people on the left.'

Another connection, however, is that *Labour Herald*, the weekly paper which Livingstone edits jointly with Ted Knight and Matthew Warburton, is printed on the WRP's presses in Runcorn, Cheshire. There is thus a commercial relationship between *Labour Herald* and the WRP's printing company, Astmoor Litho.

Ted Knight, the member of the *Labour Herald* editorial team who tends to handle the business side, says the idea for the paper originated soon after Livingstone became leader of the GLC, when they felt the need for a vehicle to develop ideas, particularly in Labour local government circles, about how best to tackle the government's spending cuts. 'We had been through the experience of the *Socialist Organiser*, when we had lost control of that primarily because we weren't prepared to join factions within the Labour Party.' (That paper, like *London Labour Briefing* subsequently, had been organised around open-door editorial meetings which were susceptible to take-over.) 'So we were quite determined we weren't going to have that sort of position. If we were going to have a paper, then we were certainly going to control the editorial side ourselves, but open the pages of the paper to as wide an audience participation as was possible on the left of the party, with a certain guarantee that, if you wrote an article we didn't agree with, then you wouldn't have a full page denouncing you as a traitor to the working class . . .'

Knight says that he secured enough promises of financial support from people in the Labour Party to fall back on if the paper ran into difficulties. He then touted around printers and found that the best commercial deal available was with the *News Line*, which also had attractive facilities for colour printing. Knight says that *Labour Herald* has a normal three-months credit arrangement with its printers. Sales of the paper are around 5,000 which, at 20p a copy, yields £1,000 per issue; but this is topped up with

Livingstone, Matthew Warburton and Ted Knight launch *Labour Herald*, September 4, 1981 (*Morning Star*)

donations from subscribers and a little trades union advertising. Knight says the bulk of this revenue goes to pay the printing bill, although he is reluctant to give precise information on the grounds that it is a commercial confidence and that he is 'not prepared to facilitate witch-hunting inside the Labour Party'. The rest of the income goes to pay the single member of editorial staff and office charges. Knight says *Labour Herald* just about breaks even on this basis.

Livingstone says he assumes that Astmoor Litho is making a profit on the deal: the company had been set up in an assisted area with a large regional development grant from the Government and the benefit of modern technology, so its prices were very competitive. *Labour Herald* itself survived because it was produced 'by dedicated fanatics like myself who don't take any money out of it . . . No one who works in Fleet Street can imagine how a left press operates. I think the only way this gets attention is because I'm involved in it. If you were to take *Militant* or any of the others that are sold, what they exist on is a subvention in terms of time and energy and working for nothing that everybody makes because of political commitment.' Livingstone says he has always previously

Fleet Street's three favourite bogeymen gather at the *Labour Herald* rally, Blackpool Conference, October 1982 (*Camera Press*)

had his election addresses printed by *Militant* because it offered the cheapest price. 'I always took a mercenary attitude. If the *Daily Mail* wanted to print *Labour Herald* cheaper than the WRP can do, we'd go to the *Daily Mail*.'

Livingstone, Knight and Warburton have successfully taken legal actions to protect their political reputation against allegations about *Labour Herald*. For example on December 2, 1983, the magazine *Private Eye* printed an apology for two articles it published at the time of the paper's launch. 'In those two articles, we suggested that with the knowledge of its joint editors ... the Libyan leader Colonel Gaddafi had been asked for, and had given, considerable financial backing to *Labour Herald*. We further suggested that the money had been "laundered" to disguise its origin. *Private Eye* now accepts that there is no truth in these allegations and apologises to all three of the above-named for the distress and embarrassment caused to them. We have agreed to pay them substantial damages and their legal costs.'

Livingstone can hardly be accused of backing Gaddafi. His attitude is: 'I'd support the Libyan government if it was invaded by the Americans or something, but I honestly don't know enough about bloody Libya to say.' He concludes: 'What I need is not money from abroad, but the support of people here. You can't buy it. And if I had half a million pounds and we sold vast numbers more *Labour Herald*s, we still wouldn't build the sort of broad support that is required.'

The concept of Livingstone really being some sort of political mole or sleeper, owing secret allegiance to a particular revolutionary creed, begins to look even more absurd when viewed from the perspective of the revolutionaries themselves. The question is: which creed would want to have him? Livingstone's maverick individuality extends beyond his daily conduct of affairs at the GLC to a personal philosophy which any self-respecting Marxist would regard as a gross deviation. Livingstone's explanation of the roots of his political beliefs must surely convince all but the most hard-bitten conspiracy theorists that he is his own man. It begins on the prehistoric savannahs of fifteen million years BC.

'I tend to look at modern politics through the perspective of animal behaviour and anthropology which, I should imagine, accounts for why I approach some things differently from other politicians,' he says. 'Most politicians come through the arts and about the best they'll get is a smattering of something like social sciences. But I look on us and our problems today from the viewpoint of how we have developed over the last few million years . . . What is recognisably either our ancestor or something very similar to it is Ramapithecus. This is the beast that comes down from the trees about fifteen million years ago and goes out on to the savannahs to fill an ecological niche which isn't being filled by anything else . . . It is basically an ape which develops the ability to walk upright; and its diet consists of gathering seeds, nuts, insects, anything small that it can catch. It's out of that that you get the development of Homo habilis, which is very recognisably close to

"What? What? Oh yes I'm Tony Benn. Once EVERYONE knew my name – I was the star of party conferences – the hero of the Left – a household word . . . er . . . er . . ." *Sunday Express*, January 9, 1983

humans, and, over the last million and a half years, Homo erectus, which is so similar to us that if you actually saw a shaved Homo erectus and a shaved present-day human you wouldn't really be able to tell the difference. One would have a slightly smaller skull than the other and that's about it . . . So you've got fifteen million years in the evolution of an animal which exists in small kinship groups, perhaps half a dozen, perhaps as many as thirty, all closely interrelated and interlinked. They move around and they operate cooperatively. Because child-bearing means that the females can't run as fast as the males, the males gradually develop the ability to hunt and hunting comes to provide perhaps as much as thirty per cent of the food intake of the group. The females have the body of knowledge about where all the nuts, berries and tubers can be gathered at the right time of year. So you are talking about a very together, well-organised and sophisticated proto-culture. You can still see all the basic elements of it there in the hunter-gatherer societies today . . . [such as] the Bushmen of the Kalahari. It is fascinating. The Kalahari must be the most inhospitable general environment for humankind to have moved into. Yet the Bushmen would consider a twenty-hour working week a tyranny because they are so well-integrated with their environment that they can exist by picking up the food which they know when and where to discover. It is inconceivable to them that they should actually bother to plant anything because that's going to be much less productive than gathering what falls around them if they know where to look for it. Unlike all the societies which have swept away hunter-gatherer groups, the bulk of their time is devoted to what we would consider a life of idle luxury – music, dancing, relating to each other, the constant flow of conversation . . . And simply because you've got such a degree of abundance, you have no real pressures. In many of the hunter-gatherer societies there is no word for war. The concept of having to fight to gain a territory is nonsense because the territory you are in supplies all your needs. So you've got a human population in balance with the environment.'

Livingstone does not take sides in the debate about the exact point in the evolution from the apes that present-day human beings emerged. Whenever it was, it was long before any departure was made from this basic hunter-gatherer pattern of society. 'So everything we are has emerged from the hunter-gatherer tradition. All of our ability, the development of our intellect, all of our early culture grows out of those kinship groups operating overwhelmingly in a cooperative way – although undoubtedly there were exceptions . . . The hunter-gatherer is what humanity is . . .'

This then is Livingstone's picture of life before the Fall. He believes that the natural social patterns of humankind were distorted twenty thousand years ago by the spontaneous development of agriculture at various places around the world, which had fundamental repercussions for population growth and social organisation.

The hunter-gatherers' dietary and social patterns had made it unlikely that the human population would have grown much beyond ten million. 'Hunter-gatherers have a basic diet which means you can't wean children easily. It's all hard scrunchy stuff.

Livingstone searches for the Missing Link, King's Cross, October 1982
(*GLC*)

There's no animals' milk or mushy foods . . . In a hunter-gatherer
society where a child is going to breastfeed for years, that breast-
feeding generally prevents the female producing another child.
Now once you start to get the early development of agriculture and
we start experimenting with maize and corn and rice, you suddenly get a dramatic increase in population. Even if you're going to

wean the child just one year earlier, you're talking about perhaps being able to double the population in the space of under one hundred years. . . . . Humanity gets on a treadmill from which we still have not really got off.'

So the development of agriculture disrupted the equilibrium of the human race in its environment; but it also brought new diseases and it changed social relationships through the creation of surpluses and wealth, the development of technology and the growth of hierarchical power structures. 'I suppose I perceive us as in a period of transition, having developed a technology which we haven't yet developed the skills to control and properly operate. If you look at the way the City of London works, it is operating in exactly the same way as the most primitive of those societies based on agriculture twenty thousand years ago. The basic motive force is greed and exploitation, which is there from the start once you move away from that cooperative group. We haven't learned to cope with surpluses and distribute them without greed becoming the major motive factor and the desire for power over others. I do not think that is a natural state for humankind to be in. I think we developed as a cooperative animal . . . and have been forced to live in a competitive world.

'I'm not saying: wouldn't it be nice if we could all go back to being hunter-gatherers. You'd have to kill off ninety-nine per cent of the population to be able to do that. You can't go back. Our problem is how to cope with what we have become . . . We haven't really broken away from the initial problems of how an animal that has evolved cooperatively copes with surplus and organisation. We're repeating the same mistakes, I'm sure, that were being made in those first civilisations twenty thousand years ago.'

For a generation which has been brought up on Harold Wilson's phrase that 'a week is a long time in politics', Livingstone's view that 'twenty thousand years is a desperately short period' may come as a jolt. But, he says, this perception is at the roots of his political philosophy.

'I'd reject the concept of 1930s socialists, which you get encapsulated in H. G. Wells's *History of the World*, where life starts as bacteria floating around in the sea and there is this upward progression through amphibians and reptiles, to mammals, to apes, to man; and then man actually continues that progress. This is an underlying current in a lot of socialism. It is there amongst the Fabians before the last war. It's there in the thinking of a lot of people around Stalin – the idea that man is getting better, that we are part of this inevitable upward progress. We're not really. We're still trying to adjust to the changes that came over us twenty thousand years ago . . .

'Individuals have become isolated in society. The Marxist concept of alienation is very much based around the workplace. But the real problem of alienation in society is much wider than that. Vast numbers of people live alone with isolated people around them . . . That is totally alien to the way we have developed throughout that long trek up to twenty thousand years ago. Anybody that had the personality trait of wishing to live on their own would have had a very short life indeed. That cooperative group was supportive; and anyone that went off on their own was likely to be the prey for a large animal, or wouldn't have all the knowledge of where the right foods were at the right time, or wouldn't be supported when ill. So over fifteen million years, as we were evolving, all the individualistic traits would have rapidly run into the ground and become extinct in the next generation. It would have been the cooperative humans that survived. Now we've got a society where people have become isolated from a very supportive group . . .

'It always strikes me when I'm canvassing, the number of people isolated on their own. One night Kate canvassed this man. She said: are you voting Labour? He said: I would, but I'm going to die before the election. He'd been told he had very advanced cancer . . . She went in and was chatting to him. It transpired that there was no one else he had spoken to. He didn't have any friends. His family were all moved, dead or gone. He was an old man facing death. He'd known he was dying for a week and the first person he could find to tell was the Labour Party canvasser knocking at the door. That is a particularly tragic example; but actually it's repeated all the time. The isolation you get in society, particularly urban society, where people are frightened and embarrassed to turn to other people for support, means that we are living in a way which is completely at odds with the best part of fifteen million years of evolution which turned us into what we are.'

In addition to this anthropological strand to his philosophy, Livingstone draws on a zoological analogy. He is totally dismissive of the Desmond Morris school of writers who draw lessons from the observation of animal behaviour. 'People look at the baboons in the zoo and see the dominant male controlling everything else and come away assuming that that justifies the way we treat women in society ... You could just as easily look at gibbons, which are solitary together in the sense that they pair for life and are very supportive. Or you could look at marmosets – ideal from the feminist point of view – where the female produces the little baby marmoset and passes it to the male who does everything, total child care: the only time it gets passed back is for feeding ... I think there has been a load of nonsense talked by people drawing silly analogies from particular animals' behaviour patterns.'

But Livingstone draws from his study of lizards a zoological parallel which he holds to be deeply relevant to the development of the human race. (Journalists from the popular press who have long been trying to find the sex angle to the Red Ken salamander story had at this point better sharpen their pencils.)

There exists in nature a phenomenon called parthenogenesis. It is the exception to the normal sexual method of reproduction by which the genes of males and females of a species are mixed to produce offspring. As Livingstone explains it: 'There are some parthenogenic species in which there are basically only females and they reproduce carbon copies of themselves. Stick insects are the classic example ... As each one is produced, there will be slight genetic variations caused by mutation as there are with every offspring. But because each one carries on reproducing itself, you don't get a mixing of the gene pool and a successful mutation cannot spread to the rest of the population.' In the event of a dramatic environmental change, this lack of gene pooling can lead to the extinction of a species. 'Parthenogenic reproduction was once assumed to be something that could only happen amongst species that were below the vertebrates ... Then in the 1950s the

Russians claimed to have found a parthenogenic lizard. In classic 1950s style the Americans said this was a lie and a fraud; but then in the 1960s the Americans found a parthenogenic lizard. So it's now established that the superpower blocs have parthenogenic lizard parity.

'In both cases it looks as though there was a normal species of lizard which had males and females. Then a mutation occurred and produced a parthenogenic female. In both cases, the parthenogenic population swamped the normal sexual population and obliterated it. So in both these areas now the only lizards of this species are parthenogenic ones.' The reason was that, in the short-term, parthenogenesis provides a much more efficient method of reproduction. 'Each female doesn't have to find any other contact of its species. It produces an offspring each time regularly. So its maximum reproductive capacity is used all the time. If suddenly a woman became parthenogenic, she'd have to be permanently on the pill, because otherwise she'd always be pregnant, always producing an ovum which developed without the need for a sperm . . .

'But parthenogenesis only gives a short-term advantage. It can sweep all before it for a while, but then when the environment changes there won't be the flexibility, there won't have been the mixing of the gene pool; and the species could be destroyed very easily.'

Livingstone is not suggesting any physical likeness between humans and parthenogenic lizards, but he is preparing us for an analogy. 'I think that that change from the hunter-gatherer societies of twenty thousand years ago has the same potential. Initially the move to the development of agriculture carried all before it . . . It's so much stronger. It organises people. It develops armies . . . And it is the strongest elements within it that sweep everything before them. Western Europe sweeps away vast proportions of the rest of humanity. Whole races and tribes become extinct: whole civilisations like the Aztecs and the Mayas swept aside in a matter of a few years – a most ruthless expansion.

'But unless that society can learn to change and develop, it doesn't necessarily mean that because it was able to achieve a very rapid and easy dominance it is therefore in the long run going to have the best chance of survival. The best chance of survival may in the long run have turned out to be the old hunter-gatherer tribe.'

This then, somewhat simplified, is Livingstone's theory of social parthenogenesis. 'It is,' he says, 'the justification that actually put me into politics. When I was twenty-two I had to take the decision: did I want to go to university and study in this field and spend the rest of my life as a lecturer or researcher; or did I actually want to do something about it? Unless we can get politics to reflect these sort of basic realities (which ninety-nine per cent of politicians are totally oblivious to) we may just be trundling along on a dead end which suddenly cuts off the whole of the human race very violently and rapidly. That potential is there. This very strong dynamic aggressive way of organising society which has swept across the world in twenty thousand years and obliterated vast numbers of other species, to say nothing of a vast proportion of our own species that was organised in different ways, may be the sort of evolutionary dead end that parthenogenesis is.'

Livingstone observes that twenty thousand years is a mere flicker in the passage of evolutionary time. 'It is only 800 generations, 250 life spans. We are only thirty lifespans since Christ . . . We are still so desperately close to what we were.' But he believes that the human race could be nearing a cataclysmic disaster and he says that it is this which motivates his thinking. 'It's the knowledge that if we don't get it right we may be extinct, not just from a nuclear war, perhaps from a completely unrestricted growth of population. An unrestricted growth of population, tied to the present method of economic organisation, means that we pollute ourselves to death before your child dies of old age.'

But what is the relevance of this to, say, Livingstone's support for the establishment of a furniture cooperative in Hackney? He thinks that, just as agriculture developed spontaneously in different parts of the world twenty thousand years ago, so it is possible for new styles of social organisation to emerge in different countries today. Hackney is as good a place to start as any.

Livingstone's utopia is a world in which people are able to

rediscover the biological roots of the hunter-gatherer tradition. He imagines a society in which technology frees people from dehumanising production work, in which the output of farms and factories is distributed to meet people's needs, and in which people are allowed again to develop cooperative human relationships – 'looking to people for support rather than going out and buying things when they are depressed'. It is a vision of a hunter-gatherer society with microchips.

Even Ken Livingstone does not believe he has the answer to world poverty – at least not quite. He has an abundant optimism that people can be won over to reject American-style standards of consumption. He believes, for example, that given the political leadership Western countries can be persuaded to forsake their excessive consumption of red meat and substitute it with (more healthy) vegetable protein. It is a world view which owes more to macrobiotics than macroeconomics, a philosophy in which socialism and roughage are mixed in equal proportion.

Such thoughts do not blend easily with next year's manifesto or this year's party conference resolution. Indeed in the atmosphere of workaday politics they sound positively loopy. These are not subjects which Livingstone discusses with his political colleagues. But they do go some way to explain his approach to policy. His fundamental desire is for a more participative, cooperative society. It is expressed in opposition to concentrations of power and to exploitation in all its forms – economic, racial and sexual. Livingstone's philosophy owes far more to his early anthropological studies than anything to do with Trotsky.

10 · Abolition

Livingstone's failure to be selected to fight in the 1983 general election seriously dented his popular image as an unstoppable political force. People who had once looked on him as a potential leader of the Labour Party, or at least the eventual inheritor of the mantle of Tony Benn, started to wonder if his career had already passed its peak. Was he, like the hulahoop and the skateboard, a craze that was bound sooner or later to evaporate? The problem was not just that he had to sit out another Parliament, but more that he was becoming increasingly isolated and accident-prone.

At the GLC his style of leadership had changed after the first frenetic year of the Labour administration. His front-bench colleagues got on with looking after their own portfolios with minimum interference from him. It became a much more collective team affair and, although there was still a good deal of private anguish about the way Livingstone hogged the headlines, relationships became more calm and supportive.

In the spring of 1983, however, a battle developed over the leadership of the Inner London Education Authority. Although ILEA is nominally a sub-committee of the GLC, it is in practice independent. It is the largest education authority in Britain, with 300,000 pupils, 21,000 teachers and a budget of around £800 million which is about the same as the GLC's. Political control is in the hands of inner London GLC councillors and borough representatives, but the GLC members tend to choose whether they will concentrate on GLC or ILEA affairs. Livingstone himself played little part.

From May 1981 the leader of ILEA had been Bryn Davies, a Livingstone ally on the Labour left. Then in April 1983 Davies was challenged for the leadership by his deputy, Frances Morrell, another left-winger and former political adviser to Tony Benn. At one stage it seemed as if Davies would step down, but Livingstone launched into a vigorous fight in his defence. The campaign for Morrell as leader and Ruth Gee as deputy leader adopted a feminist ticket. Their supporters argued that their election would be an important step in breaking down the male domination of leading institutions. The point carried with it heavy sarcastic overtones against Livingstone on the grounds that he talked a lot about supporting feminism, but had an almost all-male front-bench team at the GLC.

Livingstone responded in a bitter and ill-advised letter to *Tribune*:

Socialist feminists have pointed the Labour Party in several new directions in terms of how we should work with collective leadership, consultation, shared and supportive methods of working, and a move away from the authoritarian and aggressive operating styles which are so often used within the party. It is because no attempt has been made to consult the party outside County Hall, the organised left within it, or to raise any demands for policy or organisational changes that this leadership campaign has degenerated into the traditional back-stabbing, arm-twisting and intimidatory methods which I have often seen before in this building.

Other members of the GLC Labour group responded in the same issue of *Tribune* that these allegations were untrue.

Whatever the merits of the argument and the rival candidates' abilities, Livingstone's intervention was widely regarded as over the top. He had no personal standing in ILEA, yet he seemed to be cracking the whip to make sure his own man got the job. Morrell went on to beat Davies by nineteen votes to thirteen. According to one of her supporters, the episode was Livingstone's equivalent to Harold Wilson's famous dog licences speech (when he warned errant Labour backbenchers that dogs are allowed one bite, but if they have a second they may find that their licences are not renewed). Livingstone had tried to exercise his authority and failed. His leadership of the GLC was not at risk, but his stature within County Hall was diminished.

A more serious threat was that Livingstone's brand of politics began to look out of place in the new atmosphere of studied harmony which descended on the Labour Party after its general election defeat in June 1983. His style had been to straddle hard

Neil Kinnock visits County Hall for the first time since becoming Leader of the Labour Party, November 30, 1983. Left to right: Bill Bush (head of Labour secretariat), Tony Banks (GLC Arts Chairman and MP for Newham North-West), Illtyd Harrington, Harvey Hinds (GLC Chairman), Kinnock, John Cunningham (Shadow Environment Secretary), Livingstone, Nita Clarke, John Carr (Staff Committee Chairman) (*GLC*)

and soft left groupings without joining any of them. But when Neil Kinnock emerged as the new leader of the party, this straddling act became (for a while at least) much harder to perform. The soft left took up positions inside the ring fence erected around Kinnock, while much of the hard left outside Parliament resumed their traditional hobby of attacking the leadership. Livingstone found himself in a no-man's-land. He took care to say nice words about Kinnock in public and maintained that the party leadership issue had been settled for a generation; but it was clear that Livingstone was going to remain one of Kinnock's problems when debate began within the party about how its policies should develop.

Livingstone's own view of the coming struggles in the Labour Party will be explained later. The point which came across during the Kinnock honeymoon period of late 1983 was that Livingstone's political momentum had faltered. The word most often used about him by the young party apparatchiks who stay up too

Livingstone embraced by show business in the shape of Janet Street-Porter, London Weekend's 'After Midnight' show, October 1983 (*LWT*)

late in bars at party conferences was that he was 'marginalised', that he had become peripheral to issues of power in the party.

There was a third setback for Livingstone during this period. He was wrong-footed over a somewhat half-hearted attempt to stand for the Labour Party NEC. He told his local party in Paddington that he would like to be its delegate to the 1983 Labour conference in Brighton if and only if he became an NEC candidate. The Paddington party, meeting while he was absent at a GLC council debate, gave him a derisory vote and sent someone else. Without being a delegate, Livingstone could not be a candidate, whether he wanted to be or not. (He says in the end he didn't.) At conference David Blunkett, leader of Sheffield council, was voted on to the NEC, extending his local government power base into the wider party network. Blunkett, not Livingstone, became the left-wing council activist at the top of the party tree.

Over the next few months Livingstone participated as a presenter on a London Weekend Television late-night chat show with Janet Street-Porter. Why, older members of the party establishment asked, did he not quit politics and go full-time into show business where he so obviously belonged?

But Livingstone's political career was not over. Instead he was preparing for the biggest political campaign of his life – a fight to save the GLC from extinction.

The Thatcher Government had approached the 1983 general election with a threadbare record on all its local government policies. Attempts to find a way to fulfil previous manifesto promises to abolish domestic rates had failed because Ministers could discover no alternative local tax acceptable to them. The obvious long-term option – a local income tax – was rejected for fear of giving the likes of Ken Livingstone a new buoyant source of revenue. The drive to reduce English local authorities' spending by use of grant penalties (described in Chapter 6) had also foundered because of the resolve of many Labour councils to withstand the pain of huge rate increases rather than cut services.

In the rush to prepare the Conservatives' 1983 manifesto

Margaret Thatcher and her party chairman Cecil Parkinson pulled down from the shelf the only two ideas ready to hand to 'do something' about the rates. The first was abolition of the GLC and the six metropolitan counties (Greater Manchester, Merseyside, South Yorkshire, Tyne and Wear, West Midlands and West Yorkshire) – a plan which had been approved in outline by a Cabinet committee under William (now Lord) Whitelaw, but which had not yet been tested to find out if it would work. The second was an idea from the then Chief Secretary to the Treasury, Leon Brittan, to make it illegal for 'extravagant' councils to fix 'excessive' rates. This notion, nicknamed 'rate-capping', had been repeatedly rejected by the Cabinet as at best unworkable and at worst a serious encroachment of the traditional Tory support for local freedom against state centralisation.

In her haste, the Prime Minister threw both schemes into the manifesto. Given the absence of many other firm legislative commitments, they became key items for opposition by the Labour Party in Parliament. Both threatened the GLC. So, far from being marginalised, Livingstone was brought back into centre stage. Much as the bulk of the Shadow Cabinet might have wished to ignore him, they felt bound to join with him in the campaign to kill the Bills. By Christmas 1983 a degree of understanding had built up between Livingstone and the new Shadow Environment Secretary, John Cunningham. Neil Kinnock had been lunched at County Hall and everyone was being nice to each other.

It was a fragile unity. From Labour councils outside London came the sound of constant grumbling that Livingstone was personally to blame for goading the Government into the abolition and rate-capping commitments. But Livingstone had a campaign on stream which could use his populist talents to the full. Before developing the story of this new struggle, it is worth standing back to pick up the strands of what had been happening in the meantime at the GLC.

The key decision of the Livingstone administration had been taken by the Labour group on February 8, 1982. Their problem at the time was to clear up the appalling financial mess left by the

Law Lords' judgment seven weeks before. The Lords had not only ruled that Labour's cheap fares policy was unlawful, but also that the supplementary rate demand which funded it was null and void. Anyone who had paid it was entitled to a refund or a credit. Although the GLC rapidly passed a vote to raise the fares, it was not going to be possible for London Transport to complete adjustments to ticket machines and introduce the increases before March 21, 1982. So by the time the fares went up, Londoners would have enjoyed cheaper travel for six months without contributing anything towards it by way of extra rates. London Transport would be left with a thumping deficit of £125 million which somehow had to be financed by someone.

Ministers refused to provide funds to rescue the GLC from what they regarded as a mess of its own making. But the Transport Secretary, David Howell, was anxious that he might take the blame if the GLC decided to recoup the missing £125 million either through a further round of fare increases or by adding it to rate bills in April 1982. He decided therefore to make the GLC the sort of offer he believed they could not refuse. He secured a ruling from the Attorney-General that no additional fare increases were necessary and he promised legislation to allow London Transport to borrow the £125 million on condition that the GLC paid off the debt in instalments over five years. He imagined that the council would jump at the chance to keep its next rate increase as low as possible.

But Howell's idea was regarded as outrageous by the GLC's comptroller of finance, Maurice Stonefrost. It breached a cardinal principle of British local government that councils should never borrow to cover current expenditure. So for Stonefrost there was a clear issue of financial conscience. He argued that the deficit should be paid off immediately by raising the full £125 million in the 1982 rate demand. He also pointed out that the alternative instalments option could double the cost to the GLC because both the repayments and the interest would count as 'overspending' and be punished annually by grant penalties. He feared that the Government's real objective was not to help the council out of a fix, but to lock it into indebtedness just at the point when the GLC was beginning to reap benefits from a long-term policy of reducing it's reliance on borrowing for investment purposes.

This argument was music to Livingstone's ears. He realised immediately (and acknowledged to journalists at the time) that a decision to pay off the deficit in one go would transform the politics of implementing the rest of the Labour manifesto over the final three years of his administration. It would mean that a £125 million item would be added to the rate bill for 1982/3 which would not recur in future years. So by 1983/4 there would be £125 million available for spending on other programmes without the need for a further rate increase. The GLC budget would be raised in one leap on to a plateau which could otherwise only have been reached after a long, painful and unpopular climb.

Livingstone took a budget proposal to the Labour group which doubled the rate demand set by Cutler's Tory administration a year before. The increase was partly due to paying off the £125 million deficit, partly to the GLC's anticipated loss of almost all its Government grant and partly to extra provision for contingencies to protect the council in case the rest of the grant was withdrawn, forcing it to go cap in hand to Heseltine for permission to bridge the gap by borrowing. Using Stonefrost's arguments about financial rectitude rather than his own ideas about establishing a new high rates plateau, Livingstone won the group's support. But a price had to be paid. Only about £40 million could be allocated for new initiatives from the manifesto in Labour's second year in office – the crucial period when any administration should be gearing up to fulfil its promises. Londoners were to be faced with doubled GLC rates and doubled London Transport fares without any significant increase in services to show for it. This combination of misery might have been disastrous for Labour popularity in London, but in the aftermath of the Law Lords ruling it was hard for the voters to know where to pin the blame. By the time of the borough elections in May 1982, the rate and fare increases were overshadowed by the national political crisis of the Falklands war.

From that point on, Livingstone's GLC had no really difficult financial decisions to make. In rating terms it had got beyond the pain threshold. Over the following year careful effort was made to revive the cheaper fares strategy by constructing a new less ambitious package which could get through the courts. This produced a so-called 'balanced plan' which cut fares again by twenty-five per cent to bring them (on average) back to almost exactly the same level in cash terms as when Labour took office. The GLC's case was that it had a duty not only to make LT break even 'as far as practicable' (the point which had troubled the Law Lords); but also to provide a more economic and more efficient transport system for London. To avoid accusations of haste or devotion to political dogma, the balanced plan was prepared with meticulous attention to detail and a ponderous mock display of open-mindedness. It incorporated a simplification of fare structures through a new zoning system, a new Travelcard season ticket and greater integration of LT with British Rail.

LT's executives were delighted with the plan, which would increase their passenger traffic and streamline their operations; but they feared that it might nonetheless contravene the Law Lords' harsh interpretation of the law. So they brought a 'friendly' action in the High Court against the GLC's instruction to cut the fares. The LT case carefully avoided one of the issues which had troubled the Law Lords – that the GLC had a duty not to overcharge ratepayers in the interests of passengers. It concentrated entirely on public transport law.

To the layman it seemed as if everyone in that courtroom, including the judges, started out from the premise that the Law Lords had made a ghastly mistake and that somehow a way must be found to redress it by teasing out favourable conclusions from the gaps in their often contradictory judgments. The lawyers say it is inconceivable that judges should take such a prejudiced standpoint; so the layman's impression must be wrong.

On January 27, 1983, Lord Justice Kerr, Mr Justice Glidewell and Mr Justice Nolan ruled unanimously in favour of the GLC. Kerr said the GLC's balanced plan was a 'totally different exercise from the arbitrary decision in 1981 to introduce Fares Fair'. It was not done on the basis of 'a statement in an election manifesto', but as a carefully researched strategy for transport in London as a whole. Kerr acknowledged the Law Lords' ruling that LT should break even 'as far as practicable', but he said: 'No one now contends that the "break-even" option is either practicable or the correct answer in law. This could only be achieved by cutting down the present service and effectively destroying the transport system for Greater London as we know it.' The GLC had to strike a balance between the obligation to break even and the duty to provide an efficient and economic transport system.

In 1981, this argument had failed to convince the judges that Fares Fair was legal. But by January 1983, with a more modest fare cut proposal and with the backing of a more methodical presentation of public transport economics, the GLC won its case.

Kerr pointed out, however, that the judgment made no attempt to assess whether the council was maintaining a fair balance between ratepayers and passengers. 'Whether the balance has been struck at the best point, and even at a permissible point, is not a matter which this court can evaluate, or which it is any part of our function to assess in any way,' he said.

It was precisely this issue which some of London's Tory councillors wanted to test. The Government opposed the GLC's plan for further fare cuts as an unwarranted increase in public spending and burden on London's ratepayers. Waiting in the wings, Westminster city council were planning another court action against the GLC as soon as it passed its 1983 budget, to challenge the 'reasonableness' of extra spending on transport subsidies.

This was the point at which Livingstone reaped the political reward for pushing up the GLC rate so high in 1982. By paying off the whole £125 million Fares Fair deficit in the 1982 budget, the GLC Labour group had £125 million to play with in 1983 without a further increase in the rate. This margin of financial slack was sufficient to provide for the balanced plan fare reductions (£81 million), a sevenfold expansion in the programme of the women's committee (£7 million) and extra support for the Greater London Enterprise Board to create jobs through grants, loans and acquisitions (£30 million).

The result was that even after inflation and the loss of the last vestiges of Government rate support grant, the GLC rate in 1983 went up by only fourteen per cent. This was enough to finance a phenomenal growth in planned spending on subsidies and services of twenty-eight per cent at a time when every other council in the land was being squeezed by the Government to make cuts. So Livingstone's GLC drove a coach and horses through Heseltine's controls.

The apparent modesty of the fourteen per cent rate increase should have made no difference to the validity of a challenge by Westminster council to the reasonableness of a new round of fare cuts. But, whatever the legal merits of their case, the Westminster councillors realised that the GLC had cut the political ground from under them. Livingstone was now offering cheaper fares and low rate increases. It would do the Tories no good to mix it with him in the courts. The 1983 budget went through without legal challenge and with barely a murmur of popular protest. And by February 1984 Livingstone was able to forecast that the GLC's 1984 rate could be cut by 6 per cent without any important sacrifices of achievable policy objectives.

So the Livingstone administration escaped the difficult political decisions which faced almost every other Labour authority during the period of the Thatcher governments. Most Labour councillors had to strike a balance between what appeared to them to be unacceptable cuts in spending on services and intolerable rate increases. They remained prisoners of the rate support grant system. If they failed to make the cuts required by government, they would be penalised by the loss of grant and their ratepayers would have to pick up the bill. These penalties were made tougher year by year to make it impossible for councils receiving grants to escape the government's financial squeeze. By budgeting to lose all its rate support grant early on, the GLC escaped from the system. Indeed its main financial problem was the exact opposite of the one faced by other councils. Persistently the GLC committees failed to spend the allocations for which they had budgeted. Hard as they tried, they just could not shift the money fast enough.

In a private report to the policy committee (Labour's collective

Cummings

R.I.P.

BRITISH
DEMOCRACY

KARL MARX

THIS STONE PAID FOR BY
RATEPAYERS OF LONDON

WREATH PAID FOR
BY RATEPAYERS OF
OF LONDON

RED KEN

Daily Express, March 4, 1983

leadership group), Livingstone complained in December 1983:
'There is a general problem of underspending on agreed programmes in 1983/4, as there was in 1982/3. This is most serious
in those newly-established programmes which have quite rightly
attracted major funding but which are seeking to implement
complex policies from a standing start ... We must introduce
procedures which will make such underspending against budget
less likely to occur.' He listed a series of ideas for using up the
unspent money which, in the first half of the 1983/4 financial year,
amounted to five per cent of the revenue budget and twenty-three
per cent of the capital budget. It must be concluded that for the
GLC the problem was not lack of cash but lack of speed and
organisation in making the practical arrangements for growth.
The gulf between high rate levels and low actual achievement
levels was a serious failing, but one for which no political price had
to be paid.

In political terms the big area of difficulty was not the total
amount of money spent, but the way in which a small fraction of it
was distributed by way of grants to voluntary organisations. The
one issue which the Tory opposition succeeded in getting across
to the electorate was that the Livingstone administration was

giving unprecedented financial support to women's groups, ethnic minority groups, gays and other campaigners against the white, male, heterosexual order in society. Week by week stories appeared in the press ridiculing or condemning grants to bodies with exotic-sounding titles. The all-time favourite was Babies Against the Bomb (the name chosen for a disarmament campaign organised by a group of mothers who brought their infants along to meetings).

Conservative criticism of GLC grants capitalised on popular prejudices against gays, lesbians and blacks. Since these prejudices appeared to be particularly strong among the white working class, this brought the GLC into disrepute in many bedrock Labour areas. The disaffection of Labour voters became a major reason for criticism of the GLC within the Labour Party, especially outside London in areas where 'traditional' socialist values had not had to come to terms with the demands of the women's movement and the increased aspirations of disadvantaged minorities.

The argument within the party was not that it was wrong for the GLC to fund these groups, but that it was politically imprudent: policies which could not carry the working class with them should, it was argued, be shelved until the class was ready for them. Although Livingstone himself had little to do with most of the controversial GLC grants decisions, this was an argument he was prepared to meet head on. 'The Labour Party is no doubt going to win votes by supporting for example the re-introduction of hanging and deporting all black people. That isn't really what we're there to do,' he says. 'I think politics is not just looking at what is the most popular position to take and then taking it. Granted some people come into politics because they want to line their pockets; others because they want a nice comfortable job. I came into politics because I wish to change society. And that means changing the hearts and minds of people. You start from an unpopular position and you plug away consistently. If you're right, eventually you win. I've no doubt at all that by the end of this century, if we continue to fight for it, we will be living in a Britain where there will be complete tolerance towards sexual preference . . . If the leadership of the party, as one of their standard positions, argue for women's rights, gay rights and a proper equal opportunities policy for blacks, we'll eventually change attitudes nationally.' In this context, the GLC's grants policy was not a blunder. Like the Irish issue, it was a clear expression of Livingstone's political approach.

The Conservatives made capital out of attacking controversial grants, but they also feared the effectiveness of the programme as a whole. By Christmas 1983, the GLC had funded more than 1,000 voluntary organisations and its annual grants budget was running at nearly £40 million a year. The Tories began to worry that Labour had invented a piece of political machinery capable of delivering large blocks of votes at election time.

The view was explained in a speech by Richard Brew, who succeeded Sir Horace Cutler as GLC Tory leader for a one-year term in 1982:

In the May 1981 elections the turnout in the decisive marginals was about fifty per cent. That means that the Socialists were returned in such seats on a vote of below twenty-five per cent of the electorate. Livingstone is not interested in the support of 'Londoners' – that is too difficult. He only needs twenty-five per cent of Londoners – and this is how he is going about it. Leaving aside the ideologically committed, he is seeking out the feminists and the gay activists. He is topping up these with the ethnic groups and the Irish. He is mobilising the anti-police brigade and he is seeking out the pressure groups – CND, Babies Against the Bomb and so on. In other words he is going for the nutters. As everyone knows, what nutters want is a plentiful supply of nuts. And these Livingstone is providing through the GLC's grants policy . . . In this whole question of grants, do not fall into the trap of mocking the Socialists over some of the questionable organisations they are funding. It is not at all a case of Livingstone having lost his sense of the ridiculous, as some people say, but rather it is hard-headed manipulation . . . It is vital that we Conservatives do not make the mistake of laughing too loudly at what we may feel are 'own goals' being scored by the Socialists. They know exactly what they are doing and where they want to go – twenty-five per cent of the vote.

Brew suggested that GLC grants would by 1984 be providing a living for about two thousand 'left-wing activists' outside County Hall. The votes necessary to boost Labour support to twenty-five

Livingstone and Harrington at Streatham Common, which the GLC claimed was earmarked for a communal grave in the event of nuclear war, June 1983 (*Guardian*)

per cent of the electorate were being bought with grants and they would be garnered with the help of the activists. 'With Livingstone's grants policy, the Socialists are developing a system of winning power with methods not seen in this country since the eighteenth century,' he said.

Apart from Brew's offensive description of ethnic minorities and others as nutters, there was a grain of truth in what he said. The GLC Labour group may have lost votes through their more controversial grants, but members were amazed by the grassroots support they also seemed to be winning as a result of the programme as a whole. Where Brew was wrong was in attributing this to a well-laid Labour plan. The policy was one that the group stumbled on almost by accident. Their 1981 manifesto had made scant mention of grants. This was partly due to a general trades union view that unpaid volunteers take away workers' jobs, but more because little thought had been given to the subject by the politicians.

Bill Bush, a GLC official who headed the Labour secretariat, was mainly responsible for inserting support for a grants programme at various points in the manifesto while he was doing the staff work on its preparation. His argument was that working with community-based groups was an efficient way of finding out what people want and then delivering it to them. Small amounts of money could be made to go a long way using large amounts of voluntary energy. And funds could be moved out quickly without the need to set up a cumbersome bureaucracy. But no one in 1981 knew how big the grants programme would become.

Soon after the election a grants panel was set up under John McDonnell (who later became chairman of finance) to handle applications coming in from voluntary groups. It started by meeting the needs of organisations which were sophisticated enough to present a case in a coherent manner; but later it developed systems for seeking out bodies which needed help and assisting them to make applications. Meetings were arranged with various client groups or organisations. When the women's groups met, their outrage at the fact that their grants were being run by a man provided the genesis of the GLC's women's committee. Eventually each committee became responsible for grants in its own field. The programme mushroomed.

McDonnell says the Labour group started out on the grants policy with the somewhat altruistic motive of helping groups like local law centres and community associations which had lost funding from their boroughs: 'Within three months each constituency member was realising that the political returns were absolutely enormous.' Councillors came back from performing official opening ceremonies of grant-funded premises or presenting cheques convinced that grants were the best thing since politicians invented kissing babies. McDonnell does not accept Brew's twenty-five per cent theory: 'I don't think grants influence a constituency on a large basis; but they did establish our credentials within certain communities.'

The issue which neither the Labour group nor its critics seem to have clearly analysed is where the borderline lay between looking after the interests of Londoners and using public money for political advantage. Councillors cannot be criticised for winning votes by implementing popular policies. That is what they are there to do. But there is a problem if the rates are used as a substitute for party funds.

There were three areas in which the Labour GLC was in danger of crossing over this borderline. Grants were given to bodies whose main purpose was to oppose the Conservative government on issues such as nuclear disarmament and the health service cuts. A large advertising budget was given over to campaigns specifically directed against government policies. And people were recruited on to the GLC payroll whose political motivation made them almost indistinguishable from the Labour councillors they were supposed (impartially) to serve.

The amount of public money involved was tiny in GLC terms, representing only a small fraction of a penny rate; so the problem had more to do with political morality than so-called overspending.

The Labour GLC's advertising budgets included £300,000 spent on fighting the Law Lords' judgment against Fares Fair; £200,000 fighting Government decisions to withdraw rate support grants from London; £150,000 on fighting the Bill to take responsibility for London Transport away from the GLC; £200,000 on Peace Year; £80,000 on the GLC's declaration of itself as a nuclear-free zone; and £100,000 on a mail shot to Londoners giving medical evidence about the effects of a nuclear holocaust.

Individually these campaigns were justified, after careful scrutiny by the GLC's legal branch, as legitimate expenditure in the interests of Londoners. But collectively they clearly amounted to political propaganda funded from the rates. During the 1983 election campaign it was sometimes necessary to read the small print to distinguish poster advertisements financed by the Labour Party from others financed by the GLC.

Livingstone argues that any attempt to draw a distinction between political and non-political advertising is bogus. 'Everything is political,' he says. 'Your sex life is political. What you eat is political. Everything about us is political because everything about us stems from the division of power and wealth in society. There is no such thing as a non-political part of life.' So while he would accept that it would be improper to channel GLC funds into the Labour Party, he sees no other limits to campaigning activity of a political nature. 'Fifteen years ago councils had no need to do it . . . The Government went on the offensive with the Housing Finance Act in 1972. Since then councils have been under attack from central governments, both Labour and Tory. Gradually they have geared themselves up to reply . . . The Tories don't have to do it that much because they already have the media on their side. If you're trying to survive as we are in a hostile media environment . . . you've got to have some way of explaining to the people who vote for you what you are doing and why.'

This argument has taken the GLC into uncharted and dangerous political territory. The Labour group's attitude to the standards of personal behaviour to be expected of a councillor was strict, almost puritanical. The suggestion that a penny of ratepayers' money might have corruptly entered a councillor's pocket would have caused deep and genuine outrage. But their standards of corporate behaviour were lax. It seemed fair game to channel money into a favoured political cause so long as some justification could be found to placate the lawyers. The question was not: is it right? – but: can we get away with it?

The employment of activists in official positions in the GLC bureaucracy was inevitably the issue which most disturbed top GLC officials, although no one challenged the propriety of any individual's appointment. Perhaps the most controversial posting was the choice of Reg Race, former Labour MP for Wood Green, to a £20,000-a-year job as head of the programme office in the GLC director-general's department. The fact that Race appeared to be the best qualified of the applicants and went on to do a good job slicing the fat of the bureaucracy did not quieten top officials' fears that the Livingstone administration had lost sight of the conventional borderline between politicians and their civil servants.

Similarly in the grants field there were fears that councillors could not separate their role as policy-makers in the public interest from their political positions as activists with links among grant recipients. As one member of Livingstone's policy committee anonymously put it: 'There was a time when you had to watch out for the Masonic or Roman Catholic link between councillors and the people who got their favours. Now with our grants policy you need to watch out for common membership of a ward Labour party. Our people don't seem to remember the Poulson scandal and they don't seem to have read the code of practice that was drawn up after it to guard against corruption. As far as I know there are no scandals over grants, but the fact that you can ask the question is evidence that there is a problem.'

Ministers were privately delighted with the GLC's grants and advertising policy; it gave them ammunition to attack a council which missed no opportunity to cause them aggravation. Their main concern, however, was with the wider economic issue of local authority 'overspending'. The system to discipline local expenditure, which had been established by Michael Heseltine in 1981, relied on withdrawal of grants from authorities which spent over Government targets. But by 1983 the GLC had no more grant to lose. Its £867 million budget for that year was 53 per cent above its target and 82 per cent above its GRE (the Government calculation of what it would need to spend to provide a standard level of service). No other council defied the Government's rules by such a wide percentage margin; and none had such a large cash budget. The GLC contributed £301 million of the total £770 million 'overspend' by all English authorities. When an ILEA 'overspend' of £97 million was added to the GLC total, Ministers could argue that the Labour councillors in London's County Hall were responsible for more than half their local government problem. And they had no powers to do anything about it.

These official Government figures were somewhat misleading. The GLC's spending 'excess' was as much due to the way Ministers juggled the rules for fixing targets as to the council's socialist priorities. In October 1983, Maurice Stonefrost, GLC Comptroller of Finance, calculated that for the council to achieve its target in the following financial year, it would need to increase London Transport fares by 45 per cent; abolish concessionary fares for pensioners; increase council rents by an extra £5 a week; cease all staff recruitment; cease all grants under the programmes for women, ethnic minorities, police and voluntary and community groups; halt revenue spending on the industry and employment programme; make all administrative, professional and technical staff redundant; and cancel agreements with London boroughs to maintain roads, bridges and traffic signals. Whitehall officials knew Stonefrost was right when he said that the GLC could not possibly meet its target without stratospheric increases in LT fares (which the Government claimed it did not want to see).

Such niceties were, however, lost on Thatcher and Parkinson as they wrote the 1983 Conservative manifesto. The political fact of life was that the despised Ken Livingstone was cocking a snook at the Government and getting away with it. He had to be stopped. Their manifesto aimed to put an end to the style of municipal socialism which, for them, he personified.

After the election, the Cabinet rushed forward legislation designed to eliminate defiance by up to a score of Labour authorities, including the GLC. Tom King (who had succeeded Michael Heseltine as Environment Secretary in January 1983)

GLC all-party delegation to the DoE, September 26, 1983, for talks with
the Secretaries of State for Environment and Transport on future
resources available to London. Left to right: Adrian Slade (Liberal), Sir
James Swaffield (then GLC Director-General), Livingstone, Harvey
Hinds, Alan Greengross (Tory leader) (*GLC*)

thought the plan was batty; so he was switched, first to Transport
and then, in the wake of Parkinson's disgrace over the Keays
affair, to Employment.

In December 1983 the new Environment Secretary, Patrick
Jenkin, published a Rates Bill which was to make it illegal for
councils to finance levels of spending well in excess of Government norms. Although he did not name the authorities on his hit
list, the GLC and ILEA were clearly uppermost in his mind. His
plan had serious implications for local democracy. It meant that
the Government's decision about how much each council 'ought'
to spend could become more important than the wishes of the
local electorate. Granted, the scheme would only chop back
spending well over the Government's norms; and for administrative reasons the Department of the Environment could not use it
against more than a handful of authorities at any one time. But it
was a big stride down the road of state centralisation. The Bill also

sought a reserve power which would allow the Government to control the rate increases of all authorities, should the need arise.

Rate-capping, which was regarded by Conservative council leaders from the shires as a severe breach of traditional Tory principles, would have been quite sufficient to give Whitehall control of the big 'overspenders'. Ministers would have been able to force the GLC and other 'profligate' councils year by year to change their policies and economise. The Government, however, was also committed to move on two other fronts. Legislation was introduced to take responsibility for London Transport away from the GLC and vest it in a quango appointed by the Transport Secretary. Since Ministers predicted that fares need not rise faster than inflation, it was unclear how this initiative would do much to cut public spending. Subsidies would be removed from the GLC's ledger, but they would still be charged to London rate-payers.

Now if the GLC's rates were to be capped and it was to lose control of London Transport, it was hard to see how it could any longer do much damage from the Government's point of view. But the Conservatives had given a firm pledge in the manifesto that the GLC and the six metropolitan counties would be abolished on the grounds that they were a 'wasteful and unnecessary tier of government'. It is true that the Government had done its best to make the GLC unnecessary. The council's strategic housing and planning powers had been whittled away by a series of vetoes and interventions from the Department of the Environment.

What was less obvious was how Ministers thought abolition of the GLC would save money. None of the GLC's remaining functions were to be abolished. Most of them were to be parcelled out to the London boroughs. A new joint board of borough nominees was to be set up to run the fire service. A new quango called the London Planning Commission was to be set up to advise the Government on the capital's strategic planning issues. Another would take over administration of the GLC's £2 billion debt. The Government itself was to assume responsibility for seventy miles of trunk roads. The job of flood protection was to go to the Thames Water Authority.

The Government claimed that this would lead to administrative savings, although it refused to quantify them. In fact only 7½ per cent of the GLC's employees were in administrative and managerial jobs; they represented less than two per cent of total GLC costs. So, even if all these jobs could disappear (which they could not), Londoners would not have noticed the saving. Arguably, more administrators would be required to cope with the GLC functions when they had been dispersed.

That was not to say that the GLC budget could not be cut; but savings worth the name could only come from changes in policy – cutting transport subsidies, raising rents, abolishing grants, abandoning the industry and employment programme, reducing standards of fire cover and other services. Ministers found it embarrassing to argue that they were changing the structure of London's government because they did not like the policies of the existing GLC regime. If it was policy changes they wanted, they should have waited until the next GLC elections in May 1985 and advised the electors to boot Livingstone out. Even if that did not do the trick, they could have used the hoped-for rate-capping power to force Labour to scale down its policy objectives.

The argument against abolition which for many Londoners seemed to be the clincher was that England's capital, alone among the great cities of the western world, would be left without an elected voice. The GLC Tories, by then under the more dynamic leadership of Alan Greengross (Livingstone's old opponent from Camden days), played this line for all it was worth.

Greengross and his colleagues, confident that they would have won an election in 1985, were appalled at the idea of abolition; but, as is the way in the Conservative Party, they said that the manifesto commitment was right as a first step towards fundamental reform. Fine, abolish the GLC, said Greengross, but when London's local government was restructured 'a democratically-elected body must surely be established to provide an effective and financially disciplined voice and direction for the specific tasks that must be done for London as a whole.'

The Government's abolition White Paper, Streamlining the Cities, was published on October 7, 1983. It envisaged legislation in the 1984/5 session of Parliament to abolish the GLC in May 1986. A shorter 'paving bill' was to be put through Parliament in the spring and summer of 1984 to abort the GLC elections due in 1985. For its final year the GLC was to be run by nominees of the London boroughs, among whom there was likely to be a Tory majority.

The timetable for Livingstone was clear. If the Government had its way, Labour would lose control of County Hall in May 1985 when the existing councillors' four-year term of office expired. There were eighteen months left to mobilise the resources of the GLC to fight for its life. Before the eighteen months were over, the reselection process for Labour Party Parliamentary candidates would have begun. In personal political terms, he was back on course.

11 · Capital

As the abolition battle got under way, Livingstone was laying the groundwork for a second struggle – within the Labour Party. On June 10, 1983, the day after the Conservatives' general election victory, his paper, *Labour Herald*, commented:

Our worst general election defeat for fifty years means the Left must capture the Party for socialism or face the prospect of Labour in permanent opposition. The defeat is the responsibility of Labour's right-wing, whose ambition is to manage capitalism better than the Tories themselves . . . The way forward for the Labour Party is clear. We must resist any purges or further dilution of policy by the right-wing. The Left must not be demoralised or turn in on itself. Instead we must move forward to adopt firmly socialist policies which can withstand the heat of an election campaign . . .

It was the weakness of our manifesto on the key issue of the economy which cost Labour the election. The manifesto's Alternative Economic Strategy was a watered-down version of Labour's 1973 programme, devised in the last phase of a twenty-five year boom . . . Crucially the leadership failed to tackle the question of capital . . .

Over the following months Livingstone began to develop the theme that the most important issue for the Labour Party was to decide how a future government could take control of the capital owned by the banks and use it to embark on a programme of national reconstruction.

His arguments seemed out of tune with the mood of the party at the time. At the annual conference in Brighton, after the election of Neil Kinnock as leader and Roy Hattersley as his deputy, there was a sustained effort to develop unity and avoid opening up new areas of potential friction.

Livingstone's position was that, with the leadership question settled for a generation, it was time to get on with a serious debate about long-term policy. He was not disturbed about moves within the party to abandon some of the items in the 1983 manifesto which it had been fashionable to regard as left-wing – such as withdrawal from the EEC (which he regarded as politically unimportant) or opposition to council tenants' rights to buy their homes (which he thought of peripheral significance as long as enough housing could be built). The crucial issue, he argued, was the control of capital.

His analysis starts from the observation that Labour suffers from an inbuilt handicap in the field of economics. 'People join the Labour Party because they want to build houses, or see a better health service, or a freedom of information act, or nuclear disarmament. Very few join because they've got a burning desire to reform the economic system. Almost everybody in the Labour Party wants somebody else to do that, so that they themselves can spend the proceeds on the programmes that really interest them. Given the way economics is taught in the universities, socialist economists remain very much the exception.

'So whenever the Labour Party has come to look at the economic issues, it has never really had more than slogans. I think, if we are honest about it, the overwhelming majority of Cabinet members in the Labour governments of this century have only had a simple couple of slogans about the economy, with no real idea of how to translate them into a policy . . . Labour governments take office and get caught up in a whole range of good things, like restoring the cuts of a previous Tory administration, pumping up pensions a bit and expanding public spending. That inevitably ends up after a period of time with inflation rising or a balance of payments crisis. They find themselves caught in a straitjacket with the civil service, the IMF and the governor of the Bank of England all saying: the city is getting nervous, there's a flight of money out, the pound is going down and you've got to take measures.

'Then they fall back on either a wages policy, or major increases in taxation, or cutbacks in their own programmes. I'm certain – although they've never yet gone for it in any big way – that in that group of short-term measures you could include substantial import controls as well. I'm sure that at some point in the future a Labour government would run the risk of assuming it could seize

on that as a way of putting off fundamental choices, in exactly
the same way that they have used incomes policies and cuts in the
past . . .

'I think the reality of the situation for a socialist administration,
given the things it wants to do, is that it has to tackle the question of
capital . . . I don't think you can duck the issue of taking control
of banks and finance houses. That means taking control of all
the accumulated capital that exists and then starting to direct
it.'

Livingstone observes that the British economy has suffered
from chronic under-investment in productive capacity. One
reason for this had been the recent disproportionate concentra-
tion of research and development effort into armaments. But
underlying that was a century-old problem of Britain's decline in
the world economic league, due to its unique historical experience.

'British capitalism has been different from all its major competitors. Because we developed the industrial revolution first, we
were able to determine the pattern of world trade and drain off
vast profits out of our colonial possessions. That allowed Tory and
Liberal governments throughout the nineteenth century to make
concessions to British workers which weren't made to workers in
other countries. This was OK as long as we were a predominant
world power in economic terms. But, with the loss of empire and
the liquidation of so much of our foreign assets to pay for World
War Two, it was no longer possible just to buy off British workers
in the way that they'd been bought off before. The problem was
masked by the world boom in the 1950s and 1960s; and Tory
governments didn't tackle it. They carried on expanding the
economy and making concessions every now and then. But once
the crunch came, from 1974 onwards, the Tories saw that you
couldn't carry on fudging the issue. They had to roll back the
power of labour.

'Thatcher has not emerged with a philosophy which she has
imposed on the Tory party; the people who control finance and
capital in Britain – the ruling class in the jargon sense – had no
alternative to what they've done. They could no longer buy off key

sections of the workforce with benefits. They didn't have the money to do it *and* to maintain their own position. They had to push back the workforce. Monetarism had to come and whoever had succeeded Heath would have had to follow largely the policies that Thatcher has followed.'

Yet the Thatcher government's attempts to restore the position of the ruling class vis-à-vis labour were doing nothing to cure the deep-seated crisis of the British economy, caused by decades of under-investment. Indeed they were making matters worse. 'For the last two or three years British capital has been invested abroad at a rate of £1,000 million a month. That is £1,000 million a month generated by the British economy which the financial institutions have sent overseas.' The bankers and financiers had tried to get the maximum short-term benefit for themselves. 'No one in the City of London takes a long-term view in the national interest. It's a gross act of national disloyalty, a total lack of economic patriotism.'

The only way to revive the British economy was through a programme of investment in Britain. For a socialist government that could only be achieved by taking control of capital and directing it into a plan for reconstruction.

Livingstone says the plan would have two stages. The first would be designed to provide a temporary breathing space. It would involve a crash programme to rebuild the nation's decaying infrastructure: its railways, roads, sewers and decrepit housing. Capital which would otherwise have been siphoned off to build hotels and office blocks around the world would be put to use at home. Coal, iron and steel production would have to be expanded to meet the needs of this reconstruction drive; and unemployment totals would start to come down. This would crank up economic demand and there would be a danger of sucking in imports of manufactured goods, creating a balance of payments crisis. So, although it would be accepted that Britain had no long-term role as a major producer and exporter of traditional manufactures (because of superior competition from the Far East), it would be necessary to re-open, rebuild and retool manufacturing plant for a twenty- or thirty-year life during the transitional period of reconstruction.

Meanwhile work would begin on the second stage, of investing in the development of the information sector of the economy – microelectronics, video, cable – which Livingstone sees as Britain's long-term hope for the future. A socialist government would channel funds into research and development and training in these areas as part of a ten- or twenty-year economic plan.

Such a plan could not be financed out of borrowing. 'If you borrow on a scale necessary to do all those things, you just end up with crippling inflation and debt charges which pre-empt your economic flexibility for the future. You've got to pay for the bulk of that work of reconstruction out of the redirection of capital.' And that, says Livingstone, would ideally involve the nationalisation of the banks and finance houses. 'There are two ways forward and it depends on the nature of the political balance within the Parliamentary Labour Party which we would take. If there is a substantial left [majority], then I should think nationalisation of the banks is a very real prospect. If we're in a position where the PLP is more soft left, then probably the most one would expect would be detailed controls over the banks and the finance houses. We would involve them in a corporatist approach which the banks would resent but could live with and perhaps hang on till the return of a Tory government. Clearly I would very much favour the former . . .

'There's no real thinking gone beyond that. Most of the work by left economists in the party has been geared towards pension fund socialism – the idea that we should use pension funds to provide the resources for new investment. That's what the GLC and West Midlands enterprise boards have been doing. I think, if we're honest, the record of the GLC and West Midlands shows the limitations of that. You can make some impact and you can do some good, but you can't actually restructure the whole of the economy on that basis. Pension funds don't give you that degree of wealth to play with. So I don't think you can duck the question of actually taking control of banks and finance houses – and that means taking control of all the accumulated capital that exists and then starting to direct it . . .'

There is a hair-shirt element in Livingstone's economic

approach. He argues that capital should not be redirected into any short-term increase in consumption. 'We'd go into the next election saying: we're not promising tax cuts, we're not promising any extra money in your pocket, because that is a total illusion. If we generated a consumer boom, we'd just suck in imports because British manufacturing couldn't cope with the demand. We'd say to people: we are looking for a commitment to spend at least five years and possibly ten in a programme of national reconstruction in exactly the way that Germany did at the end of the last war. In the short term consumer needs have to be subordinated to the process of reconstruction. And I would sell it on the basis that, if we don't do it, even people who today are comfortably off and in middle age can't necessarily look forward to an old age where they would be in comfort.'

That does not mean Labour would be unable to reverse Tory cuts. Capital would be preserved for direction into capital projects; but there would be a diversion of consumption from arms expenditure into areas such as expansion of the National Health Service, pre-school child care and care for the elderly, all of which are highly labour-intensive.

Livingstone accepts that this analysis does not amount to much more than the sort of sloganising he condemns in past Labour politicians. (He says he paid no attention to economic issues until 1981.) His belief is, however, that this is the direction in which socialists will have to move and that the Labour Party should spend the next couple of years working it up into a detailed manifesto. He regards his personal contribution not so much in providing answers as in convincing fellow socialists to ask the right questions.

Perhaps the most important question, for which he does not have a ready answer, is how to prevent the programme of national reconstruction developing into the sort of state centralism which he abhors. How does he reconcile direction of investment with participation?

'That's the major problem which we haven't worked out in any real way. Just as there is a slogan about nationalising the banks, there are slogans about workers' control. There are no obvious schemes to pick off the shelf and apply. I wouldn't want to see a national finance corporation which organised all the decisions about investment centrally. I think decisions would have to be made at, or very close to, cabinet level about what proportion of the investment available to the state over the next five years would be going into which different sectors of the economy. But once central government has taken those key decisions, the actual pattern of investment has to be decided in a devolved fashion.'

Livingstone imagines that although this programme would be resisted by financiers, it would not necessarily be unwelcome to British industrialists. 'In the early 1960s British industrialists started to find themselves much closer to the Harold Wilson modernising reforming approach than they were to the old Macmillan/Home grousemoor image. If you look at the history of British capital over the last 150 years, it is British industry that has lost out while finance capital has benefited from a series of short-term manoeuvres. British industrialists are constantly grumbling away with complaints about the financial policy of the Thatcher government which are suppressed whenever you get close to an election.'

He does not therefore believe that a socialist government adopting this programme would inevitably be faced with a coup from the ruling class. 'It would be very easy to take the sort of policies I've been talking about, put them into the jargon of the hard left and scare everybody out of their wits. You could actually precipitate a coup against a Labour government trying to do that. That's why I think you have to talk in terms of a process of national reconstruction. Positive elements within British capital would clearly see the benefits in the long term and would be carried along with it . . . If the government proceeds with real authority and purpose, short of an armed coup, at the end of the day it's going to get its way.'

Livingstone believes that the time is ripe for the Labour Party to concentrate its debate on the issue of the control of capital. 'The left at the moment is flopping around all over the place looking for what role it will have over the next few years. We have to start to work out now the detail of what we mean by these policies, how they will operate, what we actually mean by workers' control. We have to start to develop the blueprint which can then be taken up by the party leadership . . . The first stage is to persuade the rest of the left that this is the direction we've all got to go in for the next two or three years – looking at what the next Labour government does rather than what we do about next year's witch-hunts.'

Could this work come to fruition in time for a general election in, say, 1988? Livingstone thinks it could. 'It depends how Neil Kinnock's thinking develops: whether he thinks that Labour can go once more round the old route of 1964 and 1974 and perhaps make it work this time; or whether in the debate that we may be able to generate on the left you can persuade the party that there really isn't a short cut, there isn't another gimmick to try, you've actually got to tackle where wealth really is in Britain and start to invest that wealth more wisely . . . I think that, in the sense that I have come to these political views in an empirical fashion, as all other methods were tried and failed, other people who look at the issue objectively will come to the same conclusions . . .

'Even if we don't persuade the present Parliamentary leadership in this Parliament of the need for these policies, there will be a major influx of new Labour MPs in the next Parliament whom we will be aiming to target and work on and persuade. It may well be that what you get is an attempt to go round the circle again by the next Labour government; but, as that starts to fail, then the choice that would confront the Parliamentary party would be this sort of alternative or a complete collapse and defeat at the following election . . . There is everything to play for in the next Parliamentary Labour Party. I believe we could win even if we hadn't convinced them before the election.'

When Livingstone talks about 'we', he does not mean the leadership team at the GLC with whom he has little or no long-range political discussion. He is referring to the *Labour Herald* editorial board of himself, Ted Knight and Matthew Warburton. It is not exactly a well-established power base in the Labour Party. But Livingstone does not believe there is a need for any new organisation within the party to push forward his economic strategy. 'We don't need new organisations. We just need

Capital 227

people to start thinking in hard terms about what the next Labour government does. We need conferences, debates, articles, so that we start to try and find out. Perhaps after a short period you need to bring together a group of people, a range of opinion on the left of the party, who would put together a manifesto for a government in the same sort of detail that we produced the GLC manifesto for 1981 . . . The work has got to be done. Even the left in the Labour Party is not committed to this sort of package. Everyone has just thought in terms of economic slogans – nationalise the banks and so forth. We've very seldom been able to get a majority of votes cast for that at conference. I should imagine we could persuade the CLPs relatively quickly of the need for this sort of strategy. I think it would be much more difficult to persuade the trade union block vote, but there are a lot of trade unions, such as NUPE and TGWU, from which you could probably win acceptance quickly. You would be very close to a majority in the conference.'

Livingstone regards control of capital as the main issue for debate, but he is also mounting a second campaign to reform the role of Labour MPs in Parliament. 'We have to ensure that, when there's a Labour government, the PLP controls the Cabinet. We've got all this accountability and democracy in the party. We don't want to find when the Labour government takes office in four years time and we've got a wonderful PLP, which is more left-wing than ever before, that Labour MPs don't exercise any control over the Parliamentary leadership. We want to replicate the methods of control that exist, say, in councils.'

He argues that one of the main failures of the Labour Party in Parliament has been that as soon as a Labour government is elected all the power is concentrated in the Prime Minister, who makes all appointments and is able to keep political rivals under control.

'Whilst it's important to ensure that we have a left leadership, you've got to construct a position where the leader doesn't have the tremendous power that Attlee, Wilson and Callaghan had through the system of patronage . . . What I want to see is Labour MPs starting to assert themselves and demand the same rights over the Parliamentary leadership as Labour councillors have demanded over council leaderships. Otherwise what is the role of being an MP? ... It is not an argument that we want MPs accountable to those small wicked little caucuses of evil men and women who have put people like Ken Livingstone in power. What we are arguing is that the elected representatives of the people hold the civil service and the executive accountable. It's a much more difficult argument for the right wing to reject.'

Under Livingstone's proposed system there would be a weekly meeting of the PLP at which the Prime Minister would report on the decisions which the Cabinet had made the week before. The PLP would debate them in much the same way that the Labour group at the GLC debates the recommendations of Livingstone's policy committee. If the PLP disagreed, the Cabinet would have to change its policy. Livingstone holds that this would not cause insuperable difficulties with leaks of sensitive information. 'Everybody knew the struggle taking place in Cabinet during the IMF crisis. It was reported at great length ... There are no secrets. The only decisions that stay secret under a Labour government are the ones where the Cabinet aren't told. Once the Cabinet knows something, it's public knowledge. It is always going to be like that with the Labour Party, unless it was an unmitigatedly right-wing one. Everything leaks out anyway. You might as well have it debated honestly. The decisions which remain secret have been the ones that were quite abominable – key things like modernising Polaris and the original decision to have a nuclear bomb. Those should have been debated in Parliament. The only reason they were not was because Attlee knew there would be ructions in the constituencies. There were no security reasons. The Russians knew. The problem was that the British people didn't know.'

Livingstone argues that all Cabinet ministers should be elected by the PLP. 'The leader of the party should come to the first meeting of the PLP which should be on the Saturday [after the election] and they should sit down and decide who to elect to each Cabinet post. So you would deny the Prime Minister the freedom to provide a majority in the Cabinet of hacks who will just vote loyally for the Prime Minister simply because their jobs are dependent on doing so. Then I think you would get the PLP electing the best people to those positions, the people most likely to do them competently and well.'

He also proposes reform of Whitehall departments to give the politicians greater control. 'You need a team of ten or so Labour MPs allocated to each Government department, getting involved much more in its detailed management and looking into all the areas that no Secretary of State ever gets time to do. They would all meet every week and discuss what they are doing, what progress they are making and where the blocks are. I would link that up with bringing in from outside a group of policy advisers from universities and from among radical activists to give an alternative view to the civil service one.' The advisers, numbering perhaps as few as ten or as many as fifty, would try to identify 'the radical elements in the civil service' who could be encouraged to work with them.

With all these departmental and party meetings, when would Labour members have time to do their work in Parliament? 'The House of Commons, I think, is terribly wasteful in terms of members' time. It's been constructed by governments working fist in glove with the civil service to make most MPs totally irrelevant to the process of government. That's why select committees were resisted for years and years. If you look at most other Parliaments in the world, they don't spend a quarter of the time in general debate that the House of Commons does; and most of that general debate is ill-attended and fairly meaningless. It doesn't provide effective scrutiny.

'It's much better to have a strong committee system in which you have, say, a housing committee which examines all housing legislation. You would then not be in a position whereby when a housing bill comes forward the whips set up a committee which they try and pack with people who are not going to rock the boat . . . You actually want people who come into Parliament and develop a real expertise in their chosen area. They are there as a permanent force, checking and amending all legislation that comes up, say, to deal with housing; but they are also able to investigate what's happening in housing within the Department of the Environment. They are able to intervene directly there, having the right of access to all civil service documents unless there is a genuine security aspect. You would actually give some MPs real power through the committee system . . .

'The floor of the House of Commons should be for the major debates where issues are at stake, not the load of garbage they are currently . . . Do we really want an hour's Question Time every day? It's pure knockabout, a total waste of most MPs' time. It's there purely for the impact it may have on the news that night, or the interplay of forces – who's going up and who's going down in the Parliamentary pecking order. It doesn't control the executive. It doesn't mean they impose their will on the civil service.'

Livingstone is espousing a system which would turn Parliament into a giant-size version of a local authority. The Government may be trying to abolish the GLC, but Livingstone will be trying to transplant its practices across the River Thames in the Palace of Westminster. The man's confidence is such that he does not just regard these thoughts as pipedreams. He believes they should be part of the agenda for the Labour Party; and over the next few years he means to put them there.

12 · Conclusion

Ken Livingstone is a maverick. He cannot be slotted easily into any of the conventional stereotypes used to classify politicians. It is tempting to describe him as a populist. He has a formidable talent for reading an audience and tailoring his performance to win their affections. If they are uncommitted or right-wing, he charms them with a mixture of self-deprecating humour, endearing frankness and jargon-free common sense; however loud the catcalls may be at the start of such a meeting, there will usually be an ovation at the end. Yet he can also uplift gatherings of the left-wing faithful by articulating their outrage and their aspirations, infusing in them a confidence that their struggles can be fought and won.

The ability to encourage people to like him is most effective in personal conversation and at public meetings, but it also works on television. Livingstone is quick-witted enough to be able to construct sentences which do not contain phrases like 'let me be perfectly frank' or 'this is a point which I have considered very seriously' – phrases which give most other politicians time to think what comes next and their audiences time to discount it. To most television viewers, he comes over as direct, honest and un-flappable.

He is an instinctive politician, as confident in the correctness of his instincts as Margaret Thatcher is in hers. For people who are that confident, there is less need to hedge, fudge and tell lies. It is a quality which is as appealing to the public as it is infuriating to political colleagues, who can never quite be sure what they are about to be committed to supporting.

This confidence is the basis of Livingstone's personal appeal. Like everything else about him, his charisma is unconventional and hard to classify. His south London nasal drawl is surely one of the least musical accents in the country. During the three years of his leadership at the GLC, his hairline has receded a little further

Not as red as he's painted? Livingstone gets it in the eye in the crêche at Wesley House, Kingsway, acquired by the GLC in 1982 for the use of women's groups (*GLC*)

and he has put on a stone in weight. At thirty-eight, he is old enough to be the father of some of his adoring supporters. Yet he gives the impression of youthfulness, of exuberant, undomesticated panache. He has brought to British politics a breath of fresh air and originality.

He preaches a message that political leaders are not to be trusted – that they tell lies, betray their principles, enjoy too much the perks of office and are isolated from the cares of everyday life.

He is the leader of Britain's largest local authority, but he wears the mantle of the outsider, a mantle which no doubt he washes himself at his weekly visit to the launderette. He is able to portray himself as a victim: victim of the Government's attempts to discipline and then abolish the GLC; victim of the Labour NEC's determination to keep him out of Parliament. He is a Them-and-Us politician, able to convince the people that since he is not one of Them he must be one of Us.

In all this the media, unwittingly, have been his greatest allies. The attack on him by sections of the popular press was perhaps the most sustained example of vindictively biased reporting in recent British history. But their indiscriminate torrent of criticism was counter-productive. They built up an image of a caricature revolutionary, part sinister, part raving lunatic, which it was all too easy for him to dispel when he gained the access to radio and television which press hyperbole opened up. He came over as a moderate personality – moderate, not in the politically-loaded sense in which it has come to be used as a synonym for right-wing, but calm and collected in the way he presented himself.

These were the talents which made him runner-up to the Pope in BBC Radio's Man of the Year popularity contest in 1982. He became a star performer, equally at home amid the showbiz glitter of a David Frost New Year's Eve celebrity chat show and in the dingy halls of the political circuit, at the public meetings and student union debates from which he says he draws his inspiration.

His ability to win over potentially hostile audiences was seen to best effect as the GLC began its campaign against threatened abolition. Livingstone visited all the party conferences in the autumn of 1983. His fringe meetings at the Liberal and SDP assemblies produced reactions bordering on adulation from younger delegates and were instrumental in moving the Alliance parties towards outright opposition to the Government's plans. Like many of his initiatives, the idea for the party conference roadshow did not come from him – in this case, the credit goes to his press officer, Nita Clarke – but it is hard to imagine anyone else in British politics pulling it off with so much aplomb.

If Livingstone's style were all there was to him, it might indeed be accurate to categorise him as a populist. But there is a sharp contrast between the style and the content of his politics. Whereas the populist chooses to advance policies which are in tune with the gut instincts of the poeple, Livingstone has persistently promoted causes which are unpopular with the electorate in general and with his own party in particular. His high-profile support for the rights of gays and ethnic minorities, and his interventions in favour of Sinn Fein and the PLO, cannot be dismissed as mere pandering to the mood of the particular left-wing groupings on which he relies for backing from time to time. It is impossible to spend any time with Livingstone without being convinced that he does indeed boil with outrage at the record of British colonialism in Ireland, at the racism he sees around him in London, at the intolerance shown to gays and lesbians.

Livingstone believes that in the long term the Labour Party can build a stronger Parliamentary majority if it can become a vehicle for the aspirations of the women's movement and of disadvantaged minorities. He envisages that they will be welded together with the traditional labour movement to form an unstoppable electoral force. In the short term, however, he acknowledges that GLC policies towards women, gays and blacks have produced deep hostility from important sections of the working class. Yet he does not for a moment see that as a reason to tread more softly. He wants to change society and he believes that involves raising the temperature of the debate and altering popular attitudes. Livingstone may have the style of a populist, but he is at heart a radical evangelist who believes he can convert the people to his way of thinking.

It is fascinating to speculate whether his personal attractiveness could win more votes for Labour than his espousal of unpopular causes might lose. That would have been one of the more interesting tests of the GLC elections in May 1985 which the Government intends to cancel as part of its plans to abolish the GLC.

It is not the only test that Livingstone has been saved from facing as a result of events beyond his control. At key points during his GLC administration, when his leadership might have been threatened by division in Labour's ranks, he was rescued by external forces. The left had won power in 1981 with a determination to adhere rigidly to their manifesto and avoid the trimming and backsliding for which they condemned previous Labour regimes. Constancy was their main article of faith. Livingstone, as leader, had to satisfy this commitment and at the same time retain the support of the centrists and right-wingers upon whom Labour relied for its slim majority. Had it not been for the Law Lords' decision to outlaw the Fares Fair policy, which substantially scaled down the cost of the manifesto programme, this balancing act would have been much harder to perform. Had it not been for the Government's decision to exclude Sinn Fein leaders from Britain to prevent their visit to the GLC in December 1982, Livingstone could have faced defeat or ignominious retreat. Yet it is not sufficient to say that he was lucky to survive: political leadership involves making the best of your luck. He showed great resilience under pressure from the full glare of media attention, waiting for others to make the mistakes.

Having labelled his style as populist and his political objectives as radical evangelical, it may seem perverse to point out the pragmatism of his administrative record. There were few issues of day-to-day GLC policy about which he has cared deeply enough to insist on winning arguments in the policy committee or the group. His main concern has been to ensure that the group sticks together and completes its four-year term, to demonstrate that the left can handle power. Administrative responsibilities have been devolved to committee chairmen and chairwomen, whose recommendations he has almost invariably backed. He has frequently claimed with pride that he is the least powerful leader the GLC has ever had.

This has fitted in with the left's demands for a more participative style of collective decision-making, but as the administration grew older the senior members of his team began to complain about a lack of sense of direction. There has been perhaps too much day-to-day crisis management and too little longer-term political discussion. Yet Livingstone *has* demonstrated an administrative capacity. Colleagues say that he has always mastered the paperwork – a considerable achievement in a building where members have trouble carrying their agenda papers, let alone reading them. He is also regarded by top officials as the fastest politician they have ever seen at grasping complex financial data and shaping it to reach a political conclusion.

It would be foolhardy to make predictions about Livingstone's future political career. His success has been based on a technique of mobilising alliances on the left without joining any of its mutually hostile groupings. This technique has been effective and Livingstone means to use it again, but he may find it harder to straddle the divisions on the left as he switches his attention to more mainstream issues. So far he has specialised in what may be called 'parenthesis politics' – campaigns which can attract short-term support from many groups without raising the fundamental questions of long-term policy about which they disagree. He is about to move into the central area of the battleground over control of the economy. Can the technique survive? Livingstone does not belong to any group within the Labour Party, he does not have any constant power base. He has no core of activist supporters willing to support him through thick and thin. For this reason he could be a leader of the left or he could be nothing. He is only as good as his next alliance.

The analogy which suggests itself is that of a keystone at the top of a Roman arch. Without the keystone in place, the arch falls down; but without the support of the arch, the keystone is of a size and shape which makes it useless for any other purpose. Livingstone will always face the danger that, if he is not at the head of an alliance, he could become superfluous.

He accepts that the analogy is apt. 'Without all the disparate left currents in the party, I would be totally irrelevant,' he says. 'Benn is in much the same position. When they are working together on a common objective which you are identified with, there is a massive force behind that position. When there is disunity, you are dramatically weakened. And, without them, I just wouldn't be here.'

Livingstone has a clear ambition over the next five to ten years: to build a new alliance on the left around the issues of control of capital and reform of the Parliamentary Labour Party's role under a Labour government. Whether these plans are realistic depends less on him than on the way politics develops in Britain, which it is not the task of this book to predict. He has yet to make it into Parliament and, when there, to prove that he can flourish in an atmosphere which has subdued many fiery spirits before him. His track record suggests that he can do both, but all that can be stated for certain is that he has the talent and will to do so.

Above all he has the confidence. 'Be honest. If, like me, you eventually ended up meeting so many of our leading figures in industry and commerce, leading members on both sides of the House of Commons, it's hard not to have confidence in your own ability. Most of them are of such overwhelming mediocrity. How can you not have confidence? . . . I think there is an aura of failure around the House of Commons. Given the track record of the last four or five governments in this country, you can understand why people don't have any great deal of confidence over there. They don't get out. I think one of the biggest things that sustains me is the meetings I do all over the country. People come along and they are supportive. I say what I think and then they question it. I learn from their questions. There's a constant process of learning. I think that is one of the single most important facts that sustains me. I know that, however much abuse I run into, there is a section of the community that actually is supportive . . . I know that there is a base out there, or the beginnings of a base.'

With this self-assurance, dedication and a supreme political articulacy, Livingstone is one of only a handful from his generation who can be marked down as possible contenders for power around the turn of the century. But, even if he does not make it, he will in three years have made more of a mark on the political life of Britain than most MPs who have spent their whole careers on the backbenches.

Some people argue that in doing so he has lost votes for the Labour Party. But how many votes will Margaret Thatcher eventually lose for the Tory Party by embarking on ill-considered moves to abolish the GLC and curb local government freedoms – her over-hasty response to Livingstone's provocation?

She, like the rest of us, was simply unable to ignore the impact of Citizen Ken.

Index